Catholic politics in Euro

HIS/40

Historical Connections

Series editors
Tom Scott
University of Liverpool
Geoffrey Crossick
University of Essex
John Davis
University of Connecticut
Joanna Innes
Somerville College, University of Oxford

Titles in the series

The Decline of Industrial Britain: 1870–1980
Michael Dintenfass

The French Revolution: Rethinking the Debate
Gwynne Lewis

The Italian Risorgimento: State, Society and National Unification
Lucy Riall

The Remaking of the British Working Class: 1840–1940
Mike Savage and Andrew Miles

The Rise of Regional Europe
Christopher Harvie

Environment and History: The Taming of Nature in the USA and South Africa
William Beinart and Peter Coates

Population Politics in Twentieth-Century Europe: Fascist Dictatorships and Liberal Democracies
Maria Sophia Quine

Medicine in the Making of Modern Britain, 1700–1920
Christopher Lawrence

Fascist Italy and Nazi Germany: The Fascist Style of Rule
Alexander J. De Grand

Politics and the Rise of the Press: Britain and France, 1620–1800
Bob Harris

Catholic politics in Europe 1918–1945

Martin Conway

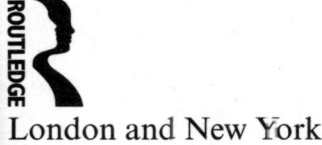

London and New York

First published 1997
by Routledge
11 New Fetter Lane, London EC4P 4EE

Simultaneously published in the USA and Canada
by Routledge
29 West 35th Street, New York, NY 10001

© 1997 Martin Conway

Typeset in Times by Routledge
Printed and bound in Great Britain by
Clays Ltd, St. Ives PLC

All rights reserved. No part of this book may be reprinted or
reproduced or utilized in any form or by any electronic,
mechanical, or other means, now known or hereafter
invented, including photocopying and recording, or in any
information storage or retrieval system, without permission in
writing from the publishers.

British Library Cataloguing in Publication Data
A catalogue record for this book is available from the British Library

Library of Congress Cataloguing in Publication Data
A catalogue record for this book has been requested

ISBN 0–415–06401–5

Contents

Series editors' preface   vii
Preface   viii

Introduction   1

1 **The Catholic heritage**   11

2 **The 1920s: expansion and democratisation**   30

3 **The 1930s: radicalisation and authoritarianism**   47

4 **Catholicism during the Second World War: a changed
   continuity**   78

   Conclusion   97

Bibliography   102
Index   114

Series editors' preface

Historical Connections is a series of short books on important historical topics and debates, written primarily for those studying and teaching history. The books offer original and challenging works of synthesis that will make new themes accessible, or old themes accessible in new ways, build bridges between different chronological periods and different historical debates, and encourage comparative discussion in history.

If the study of history is to remain exciting and creative, then the tendency to fragmentation must be resisted. The inflexibility of older assumptions about the relationship between economic, social, cultural and political history has been exposed by recent historical writing, but the impression has sometimes been left that history is little more than a chapter of accidents. This series will insist on the importance of processes of historical change, and it will explore the connections within history: connections between different layers and forms of historical experience, as well as connections that resist the fragmentary consequences of new forms of specialism in historical research.

Historical Connections will put the search for these connections back at the top of the agenda by exploring new ways of uniting the different strands of historical experience, and by affirming the importance of studying change and movement in history.

Geoffrey Crossick
John Davis
Joanna Innes
Tom Scott

Preface

This book is intended as a brief introduction to the history of Catholic politics in Europe between 1918 and the end of the Second World War. This is a subject that has been neglected by historians, at least in the English-speaking world, and it seems worthwhile to present an interpretation of the development of Catholic politics during this period based on the principal secondary sources. The book makes no pretension at providing a definitive account: many aspects of the history of religious politics in twentieth-century Europe still await study. Nevertheless, it is hoped that this book will contribute in a modest way to a reassessment of the influential role that Catholicism has played in the lives of Europeans during our supposedly secular century.

Rather than burdening the text with a structure of notes, I have confined references to Bibliographical Notes placed at the end of each chapter.

I am grateful to John Davis and his fellow series editors for encouraging me to write this book and to Claire L'Enfant and Heather McCallum at Routledge for their patience and assistance. Tom Buchanan and Denise Cripps read a first draft of this manuscript and I am indebted to them for their helpful comments. Richard Cobb, an intellectual and personal inspiration to many historians of modern Europe, died while I was writing this book. It is dedicated to his memory.

Introduction

The rituals, structures and mentalities of the Catholic religion permeated European culture, politics and society during the first half of the twentieth century. Its influence was certainly not universal. The other major faiths of Europe – Protestantism, Orthodoxy and Judaism – dominated much of northern and eastern Europe while elsewhere the position of Catholicism was incessantly challenged by the secular ideological forces of liberalism and socialism as well as by processes of social, economic and scientific change which undermined the institutional structures and intellectual ascendancy of the Catholic religion. Catholicism was a powerful influence over the lives of many Europeans but it was rarely an uncontested one. Nevertheless, the resilience of the Catholic faith was impressive. Whether it was the crowds who flocked to its many sites of pilgrimage, the large numbers who joined its expanding networks of social organisations or the even more numerous multitudes who made the simple but significant gesture of participation in its acts of ritual, Catholicism remained a major and sometimes dominant presence in the fabric of community and individual existence.

It is tempting to interpret the twentieth-century history of Catholicism as essentially a legacy of previous centuries. Catholicism, so it might be argued, was living on borrowed time. Although it retained a certain prominence in public life, it was a force of waning importance doomed, like so much of the pre-industrial folk culture of Europe, to gradual extinction by the remorseless advance of industrialisation, modernisation and secularisation. This teleological perspective is profoundly misleading. European society of the first half of the twentieth century was not launched on some high road to secularism and, if from the perspective of the 1960s and 1970s it was easy to conclude that religious practice – at least in its conventional institutional forms – had lost much of its former importance, the events of the final decades of this century render such a conclusion much less categorical. The resurgence in the power and public profile of the papacy under the determined leadership of John Paul II, the new-found moralism of much public debate and the ethno-religious conflicts in the Balkans and eastern Europe have given a new centrality to forms of religious identity and belief. *Fin-de-siècle* Europe may not be about to experience a religious revival but it is no longer plausible to consider religion as merely part of the baggage of a bygone age.

Catholicism in the years between the end of the First World War and the end of the Second World War must therefore be assessed on its own terms rather than as merely a staging-post in the gradual seculari-sation of contemporary Europe. Although in some areas of life (notably with regard to social mores) its influence did undoubtedly recede, the inter-war years in other respects witnessed a resurgence of the Catholic faith. In particular, the years between the two world wars can be seen in retrospect as the apogee of a particular model of Catholicism forged in the pre-1914 era and which – in comparison to the much more divided structures of the Protestant faith – constituted a creative and remarkably effective response to the challenges presented by the more urbanised, educated and pluralist character of European society.

The three essential attributes of this Catholic faith were its hier-archy, its uncompromising doctrinal stance and its activist and associational structure. The Catholic religion was a pyramid in which power descended from the papacy through the national ecclesiastical hierarchies and parish priests to the faithful. That hierarchy was rarely as well defined in practice as it was in theory and it did not prevent the emergence of internal conflicts, but its hierarchical structure did help to preserve Catholicism as an institutional monolith. The unity of the Catholic faith was often strained during the 1920s and 1930s but it did not experience schism. The uniform and in many respects authori-tarian structure of Catholicism was in turn reflected in its sense of ideological coherence. The Church presented itself as an exclusive source of truth, derived from scripture and more especially from the teachings of the papacy. Despite some timid ecumenical gestures, it was overwhelmingly dismissive of the values of those of other faiths or no faith and the dominant mentality of Catholicism was one not of compromise but of confrontation and conquest.

Such attitudes pervaded not merely the ecclesiastical structures of the Church but also its penumbra of affiliated organisations. Catholicism in Europe had long since ceased to be merely a church and its ecclesiastical hierarchy was buttressed by a vast array of spiritual, social and charitable movements which provided manifold opportunities for active participation by the laity in Catholic life. The inter-war years constituted a golden age of this Catholic associationism. Youth groups, women's organisations, trade unions, insurance leagues and many other forms of confessional organisation provided a protective environment for the faithful while also affirming a distinctive Catholic presence in many spheres of public life.

The unitary structure and ethos of Catholicism did not exclude regional and social diversity. Differences of organisation, of practice and, perhaps above all, of temperament between the Catholic traditions of the different nation-states of Europe were the inescapable product of centuries of moulding by particular historical circumstances. Similarly, Catholicism was profoundly influenced by the class stratification of European societies. Levels of religious practice often mirrored divisions of social class and, even where Catholicism did manage to straddle the class divide, its apparent universality disguised internal tensions. Thus, for example, working-class Catholicism of the inter-war years possessed a culture and a mentality that were increasingly distinct from those of its bourgeois fellow believers.

The very use of the term 'Catholicism' is therefore suggestive of a uniformity which was in many respects fallacious. The belief structures of a Galician peasant in north-west Spain in the 1930s had little in common with those of a factory worker in the German Rhineland or those of a university student on the Left Bank in Paris. Europe in the inter-war years was increasingly united by new and more accessible forms of mass communication but religious beliefs reacted only slowly and often imperceptibly to this process of integration. Radio enabled the faithful to hear the voice of the Pope and railway excursions took them to international pilgrimage centres such as Lourdes in France or Fatima in Portugal, but the patterns, textures and meanings of the Catholic religion remained obstinately diverse and even contradictory.

Such differences should not be allowed, however, to disguise the existence of common trends. In the 1920s and 1930s, perhaps more so than at any other point in its modern history, Catholicism possessed a Europe-wide sense of shared purpose and common identity. International meetings and new forms of communication assisted this process. So too did the efforts of the papacy which determinedly sought to undermine the autonomy of national ecclesiastical hierarchies and to assert its central authority. Frontiers did not disappear within Catholicism during the inter-war years, and the events of the Second World War clearly demonstrated the priority that Catholics gave to their national loyalties. But the local particularism that had been such a distinctive feature of Catholicism during the nineteenth century did undoubtedly recede. Catholic horizons had broadened and with this change came a sense of membership of a spiritual community that transcended secular boundaries.

The expansion in Catholic political movements was one manifestation of the common trends that ran through the history of European Catholicism in this period. Catholic political action, more so than any other sphere of Catholic activities, was necessarily determined by the peculiarities of national circumstance. And yet, as this book will seek to illustrate, Catholic parties and movements flourished during the 1920s and 1930s in states as diverse as Portugal, Italy, Austria and Lithuania. The presence of Catholics in politics was not new. Since at least the French Revolution, the Catholic Church had given its blessing to individuals or political groups that it regarded as sympathetic to the spiritual teachings – and material concerns – of the Church. Moreover, in a number of European countries Catholic parties had been founded during the latter decades of the nineteenth century which acted in national parliaments and local councils as the voice both of the Church and of Catholic interests in general. Catholic movements of the inter-war years built on these earlier models, but they also reflected a new eagerness on the part of many Catholics to participate in political life. In southern Europe and the newly created independent states of central and eastern Europe as well as in the more long-established regions of Catholic political activity in western Germany, the Low Countries and France, an impressive range of Catholic political parties, youth movements, economic pressure groups and periodicals flourished during the 1920s and 1930s.

Catholic participation in politics became both more widespread and more diverse but, above all, more ambitious. The 'interest-group' mentality which had surrounded much Catholic political action in the years before the First World War was replaced by a willingness to engage with the issues of society as a whole. Defence of the Church remained a major priority of all Catholic political movements but, partly consciously and partly as a consequence of the upheavals of the era, many Catholic parties became much more active in areas of politics and government which had little to do with matters of religion. Catholicism had, in effect, come of age as a political ideology and it took its place alongside the other major political forces in seeking to advance its solution to the manifold crises of inter-war Europe.

The reasons for this emergence of Catholicism as a major political force in Europe during these decades were complex and were, in part, the consequence of forces external to Catholicism. The development of new and more democratic constitutional structures, especially in southern and eastern Europe, after the First World War drew many European Catholics into the modern world of electoral politics, while at the same time obliging Catholics to organise as an effective political force. This geographical and social expansion of mass politics also encouraged the ecclesiastical authorities within the Church to abandon much of their former reticence towards Catholic participation in politics. Prior to 1914, the papacy as well as the clergy in many countries had been inclined to look on politics as one of the many heresies of the modern era. Consequently, they had tried to limit or even forbid the involvement of the faithful in the political process. After the First World War, traces of that mentality remained, but the leaders of the Church – including the papacy under the leadership of Pope Pius XI – were now much more inclined to emphasise the duty incumbent on Catholics to participate in politics. This did not, however, mean that the laity were free to make their own choices. In many countries, priests offered 'guidance' to Catholics during elections, leaving their audiences in no doubt that to vote for the atheist forces of liberalism, socialism or communism constituted a sin. The responsibility of the loyal Catholic remained to vote for those parties that were loyal to the values of the Catholic faith and protective of its interests.

More than the instructions of the ecclesiastical hierarchy, it was, however, the attitude of the Catholic laity that brought a new vitality to movements of political Catholicism. Those Catholic parties that had developed during the nineteenth century had owed much to clerical leadership. It was the Church that had sought to direct their actions and it was frequently priests who had played the dominant role in their local and even national structures. Once again, the First World War proved in this respect to be a watershed. Although a number of Catholic priests were prominent in politics during the inter-war years, it was emphatically the laity who predominated. Catholic politics had become emancipated from clerical supervision and, to the chagrin of the bishops and the papacy, Catholic political leaders were often reluctant to heed the directions of the Church. Thus, much of the dynamism evident in Catholic political movements during the 1920s and 1930s arose from the militancy and energy of a more educated, self-confident and urbanised Catholic laity for whom political action was not so much a matter of passively obeying the dictates of the Church as the active implementation of social and political beliefs derived from their religious faith.

The organisational structures of Catholic politics took several different forms. In some states, such as Germany, Austria, the

Netherlands and Belgium, where major Catholic parties had developed prior to 1914, these continued to enjoy a quasi-monopoly over Catholic political action. In a number of other states, such as Spain and Italy, important Catholic parties emerged for the first time during the inter-war years; while in a number of countries – of which France constituted the most striking example – Catholics remained divided between a number of competing political forces. Parties were not, however, the only form of Catholic political action. The rapid growth in Catholic trade unions in many countries led to the creation of Catholic workers' pressure groups which, although they often denied any wish to evolve into independent parties, actively intervened in political life. Their example was followed by other social groups, notably Catholic farmers' leagues and middle-class interest groups, which also endeavoured to influence governmental policies. In addition to these socio-economic organisations, Catholic spiritual and intellectual movements were also increasingly drawn towards political action. Especially in the tumultuous years of the early 1930s, Catholic intellectual and student groups launched periodicals and movements which, although they often only attracted a small following, in some cases evolved into mass movements which challenged the more established Catholic political groupings.

The evolution of Catholic politics during the inter-war years can be divided into three distinct periods. In the first phase, which stretched from the end of the First World War to the late 1920s, the dominant trend in much of Europe was towards an enhanced Catholic presence in parliamentary politics. The revolution in Russia in 1917, the military victory of the Western allies in 1918 and the subsequent peace treaties profoundly changed the patterns of European political life. New states were created, revolutionary upheavals swept much of central Europe, and in many European states democratic reforms were inaugurated which institutionalised – often for the first time – mass participation in politics. The consequence of this wide-ranging change in the political culture of Europe was to increase both the incentive and the need for Catholics to organise in the public sphere. The opportunities that the new electoral and constitutional structures offered for Catholics to influence governmental policies as well as the necessity of defending the Church and the faithful against the perceived hostility of their liberal, socialist and communist opponents acted as a powerful stimulus to Catholic political energies. New Catholic-inspired parties were founded in Italy and Spain as well as a number of the new states of eastern Europe, while in the established heartlands of Catholic politics – such as Germany and the Low Countries – the pre-1914 Catholic parties were obliged to adapt to the new, more democratic character of political life. In the 1920s, Catholicism was for the first time a truly European political force, active from Portugal in the west to Lithuania in the east. It was also more emphatically modern and democratic. Within Catholic ranks, the events of the First World War and its aftermath had undermined established hierarchies. No longer was the leadership of Catholic politics the monopoly of the clergy and of the Catholic bourgeoisie. Instead, workers, peasant farmers and the young created their own organisations which demanded that Catholic parties should reflect their interests and aspirations.

In the second phase of Catholic politics, from the late 1920s to the late 1930s, the integration of Catholicism into parliamentary politics was halted and, to a significant degree, reversed. The evolution in much of central and southern Europe away from democratic structures and towards new forms of authoritarianism brought about a realignment within Catholic ranks. The parliamentary and Christian democratic character of much Catholic politics of the 1920s was increasingly challenged by more militant and often anti-democratic Catholic movements. The reasons for this change were, to a large extent, economic in nature. The depression that struck Europe at the end of the 1920s revived hostility among rural and middle-class Catholics towards democratic political systems which appeared unresponsive to their interests. The bitterness of economic grievances undermined the coherence of the established Catholic parties and provided the opportunity for a new generation of leaders to come to the fore who claimed a Catholic inspiration for their calls for a politics of order and authority.

This rightward reorientation in Catholic politics also owed much to the mood of spiritual revivalism which had developed over the previous decade among many Catholic youth groups. Movements of Catholic Action had been established with the encouragement of the papacy in many European countries after the First World War and these rapidly became a focus for the energies of many lay Catholics. Their priorities were primarily spiritual and moral but, with the general air of crisis which engulfed Europe during the early 1930s, these Catholic Action groups also increasingly came to espouse programmes of political and social reform. It was university students and a younger Catholic intelligentsia who were to the fore in these hybrid movements of spiritual radicalism and political protest. Educated in the structures of Catholic secondary and higher education which had expanded rapidly in many areas of Europe from about 1870 onwards, they were impatient with the cautious policies of the established Catholic parties. Instead, they called for radical reforms or even for a 'Catholic revolution' which would sweep away the established order in the name of the Catholic political, social and economic principles articulated since the late nineteenth century by the Popes in their encyclical letters.

The events of the 1930s reinforced this radicalisation in Catholic attitudes. The Nazi seizure of power in Germany in 1933 and the election of the Popular Front government in France in 1936 as well as the Spanish Civil War which began in the summer of the same year were all developments that, in very different ways, contributed to a more militant mood among Catholics. The threat posed by extremist (and aggressively secular) movements of the left and right appeared to reinforce the need for Catholics to present their own alternative to the problems facing European society. Catholic political movements, spiritual organisations and intellectual periodicals all contributed to an unprecedented diversity in the forms of Catholic political action. At the same time, however, the space for an autonomous Catholic politics was gradually eroded. The polarisation of European politics and diplomacy between the rival causes of liberal parliamentarism, Soviet communism and German and Italian fascism obliged Catholics to choose between different camps, none of which reflected their aspirations. Above all, the prospect of a general European war came to dominate political life. Loyalty to nation took precedence over other considerations but for most European Catholics the prospect of a war between the Western parliamentary regimes and Nazi Germany also presented a stark choice between liberal democracy and the fascist extreme right (allied from August 1939 with Soviet communism by means of the Nazi–Soviet non-aggression pact) which much Catholic politics of the inter-war years had sought to evade.

The years of the Second World War constituted the third and final phase of Catholic politics. The outbreak of war in September 1939 did not bring Catholic political action to an end and, although the politics of the war years inevitably differed considerably in form and character from that of the preceding decades, the circumstances of war also caused the tendencies inherent in pre-war Catholicism to emerge with a greater clarity. The Nazi military victories in 1939 and 1940 appeared to mark the triumph of authoritarian ideas over democratic values, and Catholic politics in much of Europe during the early years of the war was dominated by a desire to replace the discredited parliamentary regimes with new non-democratic political systems. The Vichy regime in France received enthusiastic Catholic support, while in

Slovakia and Croatia new independent states were established, inspired by Catholic authoritarian ideas.

Throughout Europe, a minority of Catholics identified with the Nazi cause and participated, for example, as volunteers in the German armies fighting against atheist Bolshevism on the Eastern Front. But for most Catholics the sufferings of the war years and the repressive policies imposed by the German authorities led them to reject the authoritarian ideas popular in Catholic circles during the 1930s. Catholic participation in Resistance activities eroded barriers between Catholics and their fellow citizens and encouraged the emergence of new Christian democratic movements which, rather than seeking to impose a Catholic model on society, wished to work with other political groups. The war also, however, revived old fears. Communist participation in Resistance movements and the advance of the Soviet armies into central Europe during 1944 and 1945 gave a new strength to Catholic anti-communism while, especially within the Church, there were many who feared that left-wing post-war governments would return to the anti-clerical policies of the pre-1914 era. Thus, although the Christian Democrat parties which emerged in much of Europe after 1945 initially made much of their commitment to programmes of social and political reform, they soon became predominantly conservative parties committed to the defence of the Church and to the protection of western Europe against communism.

The evolution of Catholic politics during these three periods was, thus, the product of factors both internal and external to Catholicism. Catholic politics did not take place in a vacuum and the actions and policies of Catholic parties and movements provide further evidence – if such evidence was required – of the profound impact on European politics of the legacies of the First World War, of the economic depression and of the rise of communism and of the fascist extreme right. But the history of political Catholicism during these years also provides an alternative means of approaching a period of European history that has in some respects become too familiar. The dominance of a 'canon' of key events leading from the Soviet Revolution of 1917 through the Fascist and Nazi seizures of power in Italy and Germany and the upheavals of the Spanish Civil War to the apparently ineluctable conflict of the Second World War has deprived the history of Europe during the 1920s and 1930s of much of its richness. Nobody would seek to deny the central importance of these events. But, if we are to escape from their reduction to historical clichés, they must be set in the context of a history of Europe that was much more diverse than their dominant place in the historiography of the period would suggest. There is a need to explore some of the less familiar paths through the history of inter-war Europe, and the important and often influential role played by Catholicism provides one valuable means of doing so.

1 The Catholic heritage

It is easy to forget that Catholicism has been the major religion of twentieth-century Europe. This is not to diminish the importance of other religions, both Christian and non-Christian. In Scandinavia, Britain, the Netherlands and northern Germany as well as in areas of Switzerland, the Czech lands and Hungary, Protestantism predominated, while the different variants of the Orthodox faith were the major religion in Greece, in much of the Balkans as well as in Russia and its borderlands. Until the horrors of the Holocaust, Jewish populations – especially in central Europe, but also in almost all of the major urban centres of Europe – formed an integral element of the religious culture of Europe, while in the former lands of the Ottoman Empire Islam retained a presence, most notably in Bosnia. For most of the populations of Europe in the 1920s and 1930s, however, the Catholic faith constituted the dominant religious presence and, to a large extent, provided the religious superstructure of daily life. It was the Catholic Church that guarded the gates of entry and departure from human existence, that marked the major events of the calendar and that provided a wide range of social, cultural and educational services.

If the increasing mobility of the European populations meant that by the inter-war years Catholics were present throughout Europe, the frontiers of Catholicism nevertheless had remained largely unchanged since the religious wars of the sixteenth century. The Catholic heart of Europe was formed by a central band of territories stretching down from Belgium and southern areas of the Netherlands, through France and western and southern Germany into Austria, much of Switzerland and Italy. To the west, Catholicism was the dominant religion of Spain, Portugal and Ireland. Further east, it predominated in the Croat and Slovak areas of Yugoslavia and Czechoslovakia respectively as well as in Poland, Lithuania and much of Hungary.

These generalisations hide, however, a much more complicated reality. The steady decline in religious practice evident throughout much of Catholic and Protestant Europe from at least the end of the eighteenth century had irredeemably destroyed – if it had ever existed – any notion of a people united in their Christian faith. In many regions of Catholic Europe, large sections of the population had abandoned all but the most perfunctory contact with the structures of Catholicism while others had espoused political ideologies such as liberalism, socialism or anarchism which rejected the intellectual principles of Catholicism and sought to combat the social and political power of the Catholic Church. Religious indifference, militant atheism and political anti-clericalism became, during the nineteenth century, powerful forces with the consequence that in some regions practising Catholics formed only a small minority of the population.

Who, then, were the Catholics of inter-war Europe? The answer inevitably is complex and must also, to some extent, remain impressionistic. Religious faith is, by its very nature, a subjective phenomenon and historians possess no magic tool by which to measure the strength of religious beliefs of the past. Statistics provide only a very limited solution. Few reliable statistics of religious practice exist for many areas of Europe and, where they do, they are open to very divergent interpretations. Religious sociology is an art, not a science, which depends upon the significance that one chooses to place on certain external manifestations of religious faith, such as the baptism of children or Church attendance at Easter or Christmas. Thus, while statistics compiled in some areas of Catholic Europe during the 1920s and 1930s appear to show a stabilisation (or even a small rise) in levels of religious practice after the declines of the previous century, it is very difficult to know what conclusions to draw from this information. Did the willingness of the peoples of Europe to participate in certain Catholic rituals signify a resurgence in their religious faith or merely the pressures of fashion or of social conformism?

The only certainty is that levels of religious practice in Catholic Europe varied greatly depending on region, urbanisation, social class, age and gender. Regional differences were in many respects the most deep rooted. As the maps devised by religious sociologists have long demonstrated, commitment to religion varied markedly between different regions, or even between one community and another. Thus, in Italy the high levels of Church attendance in the north-east of the country contrasted with the almost dechristianised character of much of central Italy, while in Spain the weakness of Catholicism in southern regions such as Andalusia found its counterpart in the strength of the Catholic faith in some northern areas, most notably Galicia and the Basque country. Similarly, in France, the traditional bastions of Catholicism in the east and west (especially in the Vendée and Brittany) contrasted with the low levels of religious practice in large areas of the centre and south of the country.

The reasons for such variations were manifold and, once established, became self-perpetuating. It would be wrong, however, to regard certain regions as being inevitably more inclined towards Catholicism. Clichés about the supposedly 'natural' religiosity of the Bretons or Basques disguise the reality that the strength or weakness of Catholicism in any area owed much to the position of religion and of the Church within society. Thus, Catholicism flourished in those rural areas where it succeeded in identifying with the interests of the population and where – as, for example, in Poland and Ireland during the nineteenth century – loyalty to Catholicism became a symbol of nascent nationalism and of the rejection of foreign domination.

The rapid industrialisation and urbanisation of many areas of Europe presented the Catholic Church with many new challenges. The populations drawn to the cities and to the factories often lost contact with the Church amidst the distractions of their new environments and it is not surprising that even in the 1930s many clerics still tended to look on the new large cities as places of atheist decadence. Again, however, it is impossible to generalise. While religious practice was indeed low in many urban centres, especially when – as in many Spanish cities – the Catholic authorities failed to build churches in the new industrial suburbs, there was no automatic connection between urbanisation and secularisation. New forms of religious faith gradually emerged which were better adapted to the more atomised and individualist realities of urban life while the rapid expansion in Catholic educational, welfare and cultural organisations from approximately 1870 onwards had provided the Church with new means of reaching out to the urban populations of Europe.

Despite its frequent protestations to the contrary, Catholicism could not remain immune from divisions of social class. Patterns of religious practice varied markedly between different classes in Europe during the inter-war years even if, once again, the picture was more complicated than one might at first suspect. Although often portrayed by its opponents as a tool of the ruling classes, the social basis of the Catholic Church was, in reality, considerably more diverse. During the nineteenth century, it had often been liberal elements of the bourgeoisie who were the first to reject the Church and who, especially through their membership of freemasonic lodges (which in Catholic areas of Europe assumed a strongly anti-Catholic character), had been to the fore in anti-clerical campaigns. By the end of the century, fear of social upheaval and, more especially, of atheist socialism encouraged some middle-class liberals to develop a more positive opinion of the Church but throughout the first half of the twentieth century the middle class in much of Europe remained divided between practising Catholics and those who rejected the Church in the name of the secular values of liberal progress and freedom of thought.

Working-class attitudes to Catholicism were similarly varied. In a city such as Barcelona, for example, conflicts of social class dominated patterns of religious practice. The Catholic Church was identified emphatically with the employers, and most workers espoused a virulent anti-clericalism. This pattern was repeated in many other industrial regions of Europe where Catholic practice was largely limited to the bourgeoisie and socialist movements retained during the 1920s and 1930s a strongly anti-Catholic character. Elsewhere, however, working-class Catholicism was far from being a contradiction in terms. Immigration from Ireland undermined the formerly middle-class and aristocratic character of English Catholicism, while in some industrial regions such as northern France, the German Rhineland and Upper Silesia in Poland, levels of Catholic practice always remained high among the working class. Catholic trade union confederations, youth movements and social insurance institutions expanded rapidly in size and influence in these areas and helped to create a vigorous and increasingly self-assertive working-class Catholic culture.

Alongside social class, age and gender also formed important determinants of patterns of Catholic practice. One of the defining characteristics of the Catholic religion in the modern era has been the all-pervading and often suffocating emphasis that it has placed on the glorification of children and youth, both in terms of integrating the young into the life of the Church through rituals such as first communion and through the priority given to Catholic youth movements and educational institutions. Not surprisingly, levels of religious practice were therefore higher among the young and contributed to the generational tensions evident in many areas of Europe during the 1920s and 1930s between a militant and numerous Catholic youth and their elders. If Catholicism was increasingly associated with a particular stage of life, it was also indisputably more feminine than masculine in composition. The origins of this imbalance between the genders lie in the nineteenth century and would seem to have been a product both of male alienation from the Church and the appeal that Catholicism held for many women. While its hierarchical structures and hostility to values of individual freedom alienated some men, it was the Catholic Church's message of divine consolation, its emotional piety and the opportunity that it offered to women to engage in social and charitable activities in an otherwise male-dominated world that help to explain the positive attraction of many women to the Church.

The impact of these trends was evident in manifold ways within the Catholic Church of the inter-war years. Membership of female religious orders – devoted largely to educational and nursing work – continued to expand and women's spiritual, welfare and youth movements were among the most important and conspicuous of Catholic associations. Above all, the piety of the Church was strongly influenced by the disproportionately female composition of its audience. The first half of the twentieth century marked the peak of a personal and emotional Catholic faith which elevated the Virgin Mary to a central role in the life of the Church and which privileged the intense, private devotion symbolised by a figure such as St Thérèse of Lisieux, a young French nun who died in 1897 and whose posthumously published writings became among the most popular devotional Catholic literature of the era. To speak, as some have done, of a feminisation of Catholicism is clearly an exaggeration for a Church that continued to be directed by an exclusively male elite; but much of the strength of the Catholic religion – and also, perhaps, part of the explanation of its marginalisation in much work by historians on inter-war Europe – lay in the symbiosis that existed between Catholicism and a certain form of female self-identity.

The social composition of the Catholic faith was therefore anything but simple. Subject to strong historic variations between different regions, rural in its roots but increasingly urban in character, bourgeois in some areas, working class in others, more young than adult, more female than male, it defies any glib generalisations. Historians eager to see the declines in religious practice in the nineteenth century and in the 1960s and 1970s as part of a unitary process have often spoken of a remorseless secularisation of Europe from the French Revolution to the present day. The term is one, however, that presents many difficulties. Not only does it ignore the forms of popular religion, such as superstitions, faith healing, pilgrimages and festivals, that have continued to flourish outside the formal structures of what is conventionally regarded as organised religion, but it can only be applied with difficulty to a period such as the early twentieth century when little overall change in religious practice can be discerned. The resilience of the Catholic faith in many areas of Europe during the 1920s and 1930s was perhaps no more than a pause in a long-term decline brought about by economic, social and technological changes, but it also might suggest that the relationship between modernisation and religious belief in Europe was more complex than has often been suggested.

In particular, it is clear that, while the effect of the social and economic transformations of Europe during the nineteenth and twentieth centuries has been to diminish the general ascendancy of Catholicism and of Catholic values within society, they also served conversely to increase the sense of community and of common purpose among Catholics. Already during the pre-1914 decades an evolution towards a new and more self-conscious Catholic identity had been evident in many areas of Europe. This trend gathered pace during the years between the two world wars. In some rural areas, such as northern Spain or the west of France, for example, the Catholic faith remained an inescapable element in the fabric of existence. The church and its priest formed the centre of the community, its festivals marked the passage of the seasons, and its statues and ceremonies furnished the symbolism of community life. Such examples were, however, increasingly rare. In many other areas, and most notably in the major cities, Catholicism was not integrated into the patterns of daily life in the same way. The basilica of Sacré Coeur (built towards the end of the nineteenth century) might loom over the Parisian skyline from Montmartre as a gesture of the ambition of the Church to direct the lives of the city's inhabitants, but in reality Parisians could, if they so wished – and many very much did – avoid all contact with Catholicism. The converse of this rejection of the Church was that those who did participate in Catholicism were increasingly conscious of having made a choice and of being members of a distinct group in society.

The extent to which this slow revolution in the nature of Catholic faith had taken place in Europe by the 1920s and 1930s should not be exaggerated. The 'privatisation' of religion from social ritual to personal belief was far from uniform and was indeed opposed by many priests, who saw it as a threat to the pretensions of the Church to preach to the whole of society. For many individuals, moreover, their allegiance to Catholicism formed only one of a number of overlapping self-identities. 'Catholic first' was a slogan often used by the more militant Catholic movements during the 1920s and 1930s to describe their sense of overriding commitment to their faith. It was, however, misleading in its simplicity. Religious faith did not exist in isolation; rather, it was defined by family background, by ethnic or community membership or by social and educational influences. Thus, for example, the Catholic faith of Irish immigrants in England or of Croat peasants was sincere but also clearly served as a token of their membership of a particular ethnic community. To segregate the religious element from this wider context was impossible and would have been alien to their definition of their religious faith. They were Catholic because of who they were; just as they were who they were because they were Catholic.

Despite such qualifications, the Catholicism of the inter-war years was, however, marked by a rhetoric and symbolism of voluntarism and personal commitment which – especially in urban areas – did reflect the sense of identity felt by many Catholics. This was evident in a number of ways. Most obviously, it encouraged an emphasis on personal piety and contributed to the surge in the popularity of devotions such as those to the Virgin Mary and to the Sacred Heart of Jesus. It also led to an enthusiasm for what might be glibly termed the 'voluntary extras' of Catholicism. Regular attendance at mass was the duty of a sincere Catholic, but for increasing numbers of Catholics this formed only one element of a much wider commitment to the Catholic faith. A vogue for religious retreats, a renewed interest in missionary movements and the success of spiritual movements such as Opus Dei (Work of God) founded in Spain in 1928 were all manifestations of this more all-embracing definition of what it meant to be a Catholic.

So too was the enhanced popularity of pilgrimages. The fortuitous combination of railways and the new-found willingness of the Virgin Mary to appear to the faithful (often to children and in remote locations) had instituted an era of mass pilgrimages in the late nineteenth century to sites such as Lourdes in the French Pyrenees or Marpingen in the German Saarland. These retained their popularity during the inter-war years (Lourdes annually received almost one million pilgrims by the 1920s) but were also joined by further Marian apparitions, including those at Fatima in Portugal, at Ezkioga in the Spanish Basque country and at Beauraing and Banneux in Belgium. Such pilgrimages were not bizarre legacies of the past but an integral element of a more volatile and even febrile religious belief which manifested itself, for example, in the crowds that surged to various Cantabrian villages in northern Spain in the 1920s when it was reported that local statues of Christ on the cross had been seen to move or to weep tears.

Above all, Catholic associationism expanded rapidly. From the 1890s onwards, there was a rapid development in Catholic women's organisations, youth movements, trade unions and workers' associations, as well as myriad other organisations devoted to the interests of groups such as Catholic families, farmers or former soldiers. This expansion of Catholicism from the spiritual domain into many areas of social and cultural life was most pronounced in northern Europe. In Germany and the Low Countries, it took the form of enveloping the Catholic faithful in a comprehensive network of confessional organisations which – in parallel with the development of Catholic educational and welfare systems – had the effect of creating a self-contained Catholic world. This 'ghetto' Catholicism, as it has frequently been termed, should not be exaggerated. Despite the often extreme lengths to which it was taken, with the creation of Catholic football clubs and pigeon-racing societies, these Catholic associations rarely had the effect of excluding Catholics from wider society. Nor were the Catholics the only group to pursue such a strategy. In the Low Countries especially, this development of Catholic associationism formed part of a much broader 'pillarisation' of society, in which all the major socio-political movements – including Socialists, Liberals and Protestants – developed their own networks of cultural and social organisations.

Nevertheless, the development of these myriad Catholic associations clearly did reflect the willingness of many Catholics to regard their religious faith as something that extended beyond the doors of the Church. The implications of this more self-conscious Catholic faith for the role that Catholicism should play in society as a whole were ambivalent. On the one hand, it led some Catholics to focus on a personal piety that encouraged a withdrawal from the world. On the other, the sense of religious commitment prompted many to assert the presence of Catholicism in modern society. It was this public and, at times, almost arrogant mentality that was most prominent during the inter-war years. The Nazi mass rallies at Nuremberg or Stalinist parades have become such central images of the 1930s that it is easy to forget that these forms of mass mobilisation were far from being the monopoly of movements of the extreme right or left. Rallies, parades, uniforms and anthems were a widespread phenomenon in Europe and strongly marked the Catholicism of the era. Annual Catholic festivals, such as the *Katholikentage* (Catholic Days) in Germany and the *Semaines Sociales Catholiques* (Catholic Social Weeks) in France, were supplemented by special events such as the Eucharistic Congress attended by a million Irish Catholics in Phoenix Park in Dublin in 1932 and the similarly grandiose celebrations held at Nitra in Slovakia in 1933 to mark the 1,100th anniversary of the foundation of the first Christian church on Slovak soil. These events were consciously intended to demonstrate the strength and common purpose of the

Catholic faithful. The parades of the uniformed youth movements, the acts of collective worship and the speeches by the clergy and secular leaders, all reinforced the image of a Catholic faith resolutely determined to assert its public presence.

Nor was it merely such national events that reflected this mentality. It also permeated the life of many local parishes, which were increasingly dominated by public events, such as the annual parades by Catholic organisations, open-air masses or campaigns against forms of mass entertainment deemed to reflect the pernicious spirit of modern immorality. Catholicism was more visible, more strident and in some respects more intolerant. The language of the Church and of its supporters was militant and frequently intransigent, eager to proclaim the universality of the Catholic truth and dismissive of the values of other faiths and political traditions. Such rhetoric should not, of course, be taken at face value. The euphoric declarations of young militants or the impression of categorical authority self-consciously fostered by the papacy were not representative of the mentality of all Catholics. Nor should the emphatic condemnations of liberal and socialist heresies issued from the pulpits and echoed in much of the Catholic press be allowed to disguise the spirit of common purpose that often led Catholics to collaborate with non-believers. Nevertheless, the dominant impression conveyed by Catholicism was that of a faith that sought to confront the modern world without compromise. Hierarchical in its structures, categorical in its certainties and intransigent in its relations with others, the Catholic Church presented itself as a bastion of truth in a corrupt and decadent society.

The evolution within Catholicism towards a faith that was more personal and at the same time more concerned to assert the public presence of the religion provides the background which helps to understand the expansion in Catholic political movements in Europe during the inter-war years. The sense of shared identity and, simultaneously, the belief that Catholicism offered a solution to the wider problems of society created an inextricable interconnection between religious beliefs and political actions which often ran directly counter to the conventional liberal notion that religious belief was a matter of private conscience. Although some Catholic intellectuals feared that the direct involvement of Catholicism in political life symbolised by the existence of explicitly Catholic parties threatened to undermine the purity of the faith, their views were not shared by the majority of their co-believers, for whom the connection between Catholicism and politics was both necessary and natural.

This conviction was not, however, solely a product of the changing nature of the Catholic faith. It was also the legacy of past history. Throughout the nineteenth century, conflicts between the competing authorities of Church and State had dominated much of the political life of Catholic Europe. Although it would be possible to trace the origins of these disputes back to the religious wars of the sixteenth century or indeed to the interminable rivalries of monarchs and clerics of the medieval world, it was the French Revolution of 1789 that indisputably marked the beginning of these modern wars of Church and State. By elevating (even if it did not entirely invent) the notion of a secular state authority deriving its legitimacy not from God but from the people or – in its less radical form – the nation, the regimes of the Revolutionary years laid the basis for the subsequent political conflicts. In doing so, they also brought matters of religion to the centre of political life. Their efforts to subordinate the Catholic Church to the civil authorities while also trying to rationalise its structures and practices in accordance with Enlightenment principles led many (though certainly not all) Catholic clergy and faithful to rally to the counter-revolutionary cause, encouraging in its turn a strongly anti-Catholic stance among many revolutionaries. The battle lines were drawn and, despite the improvised efforts of Napoleon in the 1800s to reconstruct an alliance of Church and State, they were never to go away. During the nineteenth century, successive French regimes were either undermined by or drew their strength from the emotions raised by conflicts of Church and State. On one side, Republicans, drawing on the Revolutionary heritage, exalted the authority of the state and the values of liberalism and *laïcité*; while, on the other side, a Royalist political tradition used the rhetoric and imagery of Catholicism to advocate a return to the values of the pre-1789 world.

What might be termed 'the French disease' soon found fertile soil elsewhere in Catholic Europe. Partly as a consequence of the exportation of the conflicts of the French Revolution during the Revolutionary and Napoleonic wars, but above all because they reflected divisions internal to these societies, struggles between Church and State became a general phenomenon in Catholic Europe during the nineteenth century. As in France, such disputes were both institutional and ideological. Conflicts of jurisdiction between an expanding state authority and the traditional liberties of the Church were reinforced by the cultural struggle between the advocates of a progressive and secular liberalism and the defenders of a traditional order symbolised by the Catholic faith. In Germany, popular radicals and liberal nationalists seeking a unified German nation defined themselves against Catholicism; while in Italy both a popular republicanism and the modernising liberals of the northern cities opposed the traditionalist immobilism symbolised by the Papal States and their conservative allies. It was, however, in the Iberian peninsula that the position of the Church in society was most bitterly contested. In both Spain and Portugal, disputes concerning the Catholic Church formed a central element of the often violent conflict between liberal and republican anti-clericals and Catholic monarchists.

Thus, by the mid-nineteenth century, Catholicism had acquired an indelible political hue. Despite the attempts of Lamennais and others in France in the 1840s to develop a left-wing Catholicism or of Garibaldi in Italy to fuse nationalism and popular Catholicism, the institutions of the Catholic Church stood firmly behind the defence of the traditional order and against the atheist heresies of liberalism, republicanism and socialism. This stance was symbolised above all by the attitude of the papacy. During the pontificate of Pius IX (1846–78) the papacy began to acquire its modern importance as the organisational and spiritual focus of the Catholic faith. This was a position that Pius IX and his successors used to advance their definition of Catholic orthodoxy. Reinforced by his hostility to the unification of Italy in 1859–60 which had deprived the papacy of its territories in central Italy, Pius IX categorically rejected – notably in the *Syllabus of Errors* published in 1864 – notions of individualism and of representative government as incompatible with Christian teachings.

The ascendancy of the papacy was remarkably widely accepted by European Catholics. With the exception of small dissident groups such as the so-called Old Catholics in Germany who rejected the proclamation of the doctrine of papal infallibility in 1870, most European Catholics came to accept the moral, if not necessarily the institutional, authority of the Popes. The statements of the Popes on a wide range of subjects issued in the form of encyclicals acquired the status of incontrovertible doctrinal statements and there developed in many areas of western Europe an ultramontane (literally 'beyond the mountains', a reference to Rome) style of Catholic piety which shared both the emotional religiosity and hostility to modern political ideas advocated by the Popes.

The Church–State conflicts and the stance of the papacy served as both a stimulus and a hindrance to the emergence of Catholic political movements. While seeking to hold the faithful apart from the political process, the Church also needed to influence this process in ways favourable to its interests. Reliance on the support of monarchs or of sympathetic dictators (such as Napoleon III during the period of the

Second Empire in France from 1851 to 1870) were one means of doing so, but the increasing importance of structures of representative government in much of Europe obliged the Church also to adapt to the reality of modern politics. By 1880, all of the major Catholic states of western and central Europe – Italy, Spain, France, Germany, the Low Countries and the Habsburg Empire – possessed some variant of parliamentary government. And, even if in many cases the authority of these assemblies remained limited, they nevertheless provided a public forum in which it was important that Catholic interests were respected.

The incentive for Catholics to organise both in these national assemblies as well as in the structures of local government, which proliferated during the latter decades of the nineteenth century, was reinforced by intellectual and social trends within the Catholic faith which encouraged many lay Catholics to play a more active role in public life. The emergence, especially in urban areas, of an educated Catholic bourgeois class of lawyers, businessmen, schoolteachers and other professionals provided a new lay leadership for the Catholic faithful which – as the examples of the Centre Party in Germany and the Catholic Party in Belgium which rapidly emerged as powerful political parties in the 1870s and 1880s demonstrated – was eager to combine its Catholic and social concerns in the creation of Catholic parties. If these parliamentary parties were predominantly expressions of what has been termed a 'liberal Catholicism' which sought to combine loyalty to the Catholic faith with an acceptance of the liberal political structures and capitalist economy of late nineteenth-century Europe, a different form of Catholic political engagement was represented by what are conventionally described as movements of 'social Catholicism'. Rather than embracing the modern world, these groups defined themselves against it. Drawing inspiration from both the declarations of the papacy and the writings of a number of Catholic intellectuals such as Albert De Mun in France, they rejected the social and political *status quo*. Social Catholicism was oriented primarily towards the new industrial proletariat. The rapid expansion of the new industrial cities and the bitter social conflicts symbolised by the violent suppression of the Paris Commune in 1871 led these social Catholics to advocate social and economic reforms which, they claimed, would replace the antagonisms of class conflict with a social order inspired by Catholic values of charity and mutual solidarity.

Social Catholicism was in many respects nostalgic and reactionary in character. Its marked paternalist tone and the prominent role played in many social Catholic organisations by an aristocratic elite symbolised the wish of many of its exponents to turn the clock back to a fanciful neo-medieval world of social hierarchies and Catholic piety. Charity and moral platitudes offered no solution to the social problems of modern Europe and for many Catholic employers, such as the textile manufacturers of the north of France, social Catholic doctrines provided a convenient excuse for rejecting trade union rights while imposing a Draconian moral discipline on their employees. Social Catholicism did, however, also take more radical forms. From the late 1880s onwards in many countries of Catholic Europe, most notably in Italy, France and Belgium, there emerged 'Christian democrat' movements, often led by sympathetic priests or intellectuals, but composed for the most part of Catholic farmers and industrial workers. These were often initially socio-economic rather than political in character and, as in the case of the Catholic agricultural syndicates which flourished in the west of France and in some areas of northern Italy, were focused primarily on material issues. Similarly, in the 1890s, Catholic trade unionism gradually developed, leading to the formation of the first Catholic trade union confederations, such as the Gesamtverband der christlichen Gewerkschaften Deutschlands (Union of German Christian Trade Unions, GcG) founded in Germany in 1899, which, although they could not yet match the socialist trade unions in size, laid the basis for the subsequent rapid expansion in Catholic trade unions during the inter-war years.

The development of the social Catholic movement owed much to the encouragement of the papacy which, in contrast to its cautious attitude towards Catholic political parties, approved of the social and spiritual priorities of social Catholic groups. Papal declarations echoed the critiques of liberal political and social ideas, most notably in the encyclical *Rerum Novarum* published by Pope Leo XIII in 1891. This encyclical, perhaps the most influential published by the papacy in modern times, stressed the anti-Christian character of the individualist and competitive principles that underpinned the capitalist economic system and expounded (albeit in very general terms) the bases of a Catholic social and economic order. *Rerum Novarum* had an enormous impact within Catholicism and in many respects constituted the beginning of the efforts of the papacy during the first half of the twentieth century to develop, by means of a long series of encyclicals and other public declarations, a comprehensive Catholic doctrine on social and political issues. It also reflected, however, the ambivalence that characterised much of social Catholicism. On the one hand, *Rerum Novarum* could be used to justify a nostalgic anti-modernism; on the other hand, its denunciation of the sufferings of the industrial working class provided the basis for the Catholic movements of social emancipation which developed during the subsequent decades.

The ambivalence expressed by *Rerum Novarum* continued to surround social Catholic movements throughout the years prior to the First World War. The emergence of Catholic trade unions led inevitably to the first tentative efforts to create Christian democrat political movements. The Ligue Démocratique Belge (Belgian Democratic League), founded in 1891, and the Turin Programme published by Italian Christian democrat groups in 1899 both expressed a desire to move beyond the predominantly bourgeois policies of parliamentary Catholic parties. It would, however, be simplistic to regard – as some historians have done – these initiatives as precursors of the Christian Democrat parties which came to the fore in much of western Europe after 1945. The term 'Christian democrat' in the pre-1914 era (and indeed in many cases during the 1920s and 1930s) was used to express the popular orientation of these movements and did not, as Pope Leo XIII was eager to stress in the encyclical *Graves de Communi* of 1901, signify an identification with the principles of a democratic political system. Not all Christian democrats shared the profoundly anti-democratic views of the papacy, but nevertheless many Christian democrat groups remained caught somewhat awkwardly between an engagement with modern society and its rejection in favour of an often utopian vision of a restored pre-industrial world.

The increasing preoccupation with political action evident among Christian democrat groups prior to 1914 formed part of a much wider political mobilisation of European Catholics evident from the 1890s to the First World War. Although there still remained, especially in the papacy and among some national ecclesiastical hierarchies, a distrust of direct Catholic political engagement, the need to defend Catholic interests within the political process as well as the desire on the part of many lay Catholics to participate actively in public life, brought about a rapid growth in forms of Catholic politics. Some of these were primarily economic. The agrarian leagues, which were active in Bavaria and in a number of other Catholic areas of rural Germany during the 1890s, were essentially economic protest movements, dressed rather superficially in Catholic clothes. Somewhat similar were the populist politics practised by Karl Lueger, leader of the Christian Social Party (Christlich-Soziale Partei) founded in Vienna in 1891, and who was the mayor of the city from 1897 until his death in 1910. Mixing an opportunistic anti-semitism with a defence of lower-middle-class interests, Lueger's movement, rather like the Catholic nationalist movements of the right that were active in France at the same time, exploited the rhetoric and symbolism of Catholicism without being primarily Catholic political movements. Much more clearly Catholic in inspiration were the numerous Catholic intellectual groups that emerged during the 1890s and 1900s. It was in France that these were most prominent. Representative both of the increased engagement of intellectuals with politics and of the renewed interest in Catholicism in French intellectual circles during the pre-1914 era, groups such as *Action Française* (French Action) of Charles Maurras on the nationalist right and the more Christian democrat *Le Sillon* (The Furrow) led by Marc Sangnier constituted a prominent and often turbulent presence in Parisian student and intellectual life.

It was, however, the Catholic parties that constituted the most substantial Catholic presence in European politics. By 1914, Catholic parties of varying degrees of importance existed in almost all of the Catholic states of Europe. The first to emerge were the Zentrumspartei (Centre Party), founded in Germany immediately after Bismarck's forging of a Prussian-led unified state in 1871, and the Belgian Catholic Party, which remained in power from 1884 to the First World War. These models were gradually followed elsewhere. From the 1880s Catholic politicians played a role in Dutch government; in Switzerland the Konservative Volkspartei (Conservative People's Party, KVP) was established in 1912; while in France the Action Libérale Populaire (Popular Liberal Action), founded in 1902 by Albert De Mun, although it denied its exclusively Catholic character, acted in effect as a voice for Catholic opinions within the Third Republic. Even in Italy, where papal opposition to the unified Italian state had long acted as a brake on Catholic political development, a relaxation in the papal stance in 1905 allowed Catholic deputies to enter parliament for the first time. By 1914 only the Iberian peninsula constituted an exception to the general trend towards confessional Catholic parties.

The establishment of these parties and, more importantly, the willingness of large numbers of the Catholic laity to vote for them should be seen primarily as a product of the gradual emergence among the faithful of a shared Catholic identity. The immediate stimulus for their creation was, however, frequently provided by the actions of others. From the 1870s to the First World War there was a resurgence in the long-standing political conflicts surrounding the status of the Church in many areas of Catholic Europe. Bismarck's *Kulturkampf* (Culture Struggle) of the 1870s, a largely opportunistic attempt to rally liberal opinion to the Second Reich by focusing hostility on the supposedly anti-national character of the Catholic minority, did more than any amount of Catholic propaganda to convince German Catholics to vote for the Centre Party. Similarly, in Belgium the decisive success of the Catholic Party in the elections of 1884 was a reaction to the anti-clerical policies of the Liberal government. In France in the 1890s, the Dreyfus Affair, the dispute surrounding the case of an army officer of Jewish origins wrongly accused of spying for Germany, reawakened the old divisions between republicanism and Catholicism. Hopes of a reconciliation of Catholics with the Third Republic were dashed and in 1905 a centre-left Republican government led by Emile Combes decreed the separation of Church and State, depriving the Catholic Church both of its quasi-official status and also of state financial support. The French example was soon followed in Portugal, where the overthrow of the monarchy in 1910 and its replacement by a Republic led not merely to the separation of Church and State but to a programme of anti-clerical legislation on a scale not witnessed in Europe since the French Revolution.

In these circumstances, it was scarcely surprising that most Catholic parties in the pre-1914 era concentrated on defending what might be termed 'traditional' Catholic issues. Especially in those states such as the Netherlands, Germany or Switzerland where Catholics had long constituted a disadvantaged minority, their electoral platform was first and foremost the material and spiritual defence of the Church but also of its affiliated structures, most notably its educational institutions. In so far as they possessed a wider agenda, this too was dominated by the particular concerns of the Catholic community, such as in the case of Germany and Belgium where the Catholic parties were careful to protect the economic interests of their largely rural electorates. This 'lobby-group' mentality, concerned more with the defence of sectional concerns than affairs of state, remained dominant in much Catholic politics prior to 1914, but their participation in parliamentary politics (and in some cases their role in central and local government) also obliged these parties to develop a wider political agenda. This often proved difficult. The defence of confessional interests provided the glue that united the forces of political Catholicism and, beyond a shared rhetoric of hostility to liberal political and economic principles, Catholic parties rarely found it easy to reconcile their internal divisions. Thus, in Germany, conflicts of social class and of regional self-interest often threatened to undermine the coherence of the Centre Party parliamentary group in the Reichstag, while the Catholic deputies elected to the Italian parliament after 1904 remained clearly divided between Christian democrats and a predominantly bourgeois group of deputies willing to collaborate with the Liberal and conservative ruling elite.

Despite these divisions, however, Catholic groupings had established themselves as a prominent force in European politics by the First World War. Liberated from reliance on others to protect their concerns, Catholics had become in much of Europe full participants in the political process. Participation did not, however, signify acceptance and there remained in much of Catholic politics a deep distrust of modern political structures. Rather in the manner of the Marxist–Socialist parties of the same era, the Catholic parties of the late nineteenth century were manifestations of a 'negative integration': they took part in politics without thereby necessarily identifying with the structures of liberal parliamentarism which by 1914 had become dominant in most of Europe. The extent of this Catholic alienation varied. In some areas of northern Europe, most notably in the Low Countries, Catholic parties sincerely embraced parliamentary politics as the best means of protecting their interests. Elsewhere, however, such as in France and Italy, Catholic attitudes continued to be dominated by their historic antipathy to the existing regimes. Above all, there existed a strong sense of Catholic distinctiveness. Religious, social and political trends all reinforced the tendency of the Catholics of Europe to regard themselves as a distinct community, united by their religious faith but also by their moral and social values. It was this gradual congealing of a shared Catholic identity that provided the basis for the rapid expansion in political Catholicism that took place after the First World War.

BIBLIOGRAPHICAL NOTES

McLeod (1981) is an indispensable general account of religious trends in modern Europe. Terrenoire (1994) and Boulard (1954) provide introductions to the complexities of religious sociology. Regional differences in religious practice in Italy, Spain and France are detailed in Pollard (1996), Lannon (1987) and Rémond (1992a) respectively, while McLeod (1995) is a useful collection of essays on urban religion. Kaplan's (1992) study of Barcelona and Jeffery's (1995) of socialists in Upper Austria provide interesting examples of the strength of local divisions between clericals and anti-clericals. Works on working-class Catholicism include those of Fielding (1993) on Irish immigrants in Manchester, the collection *Cent ans* (1991) on the Nord region of France and Zarnowska (1991) on Poland. The particular appeal of religion to women is discussed from different perspectives by Langlois

(1984), Gibson (1989), McMillan (1991), Rémond (1992a) and, perhaps most penetratingly, by Vincent (1996b).

Dobbelaere (1981) provides an introduction to the concept of secularisation while Isambart (1982) discusses the resilience of popular forms of superstitious belief. The emergence of a new sense of Catholic identity in Germany during the nineteenth century is traced by Sperber (1984) and Anderson (1995). Altermatt (1972) and Fahey (1992) provide evidence of the similar processes in Switzerland and Ireland. The continued centrality of Catholicism in the fabric of rural society is discussed with reference to Brittany by Lambert (1983) and by Christian (1972, 1992 and 1996) in his important work on northern Spain.

Fouilloux (1990) is a useful general account of the evolution in forms of religious devotion during the early twentieth century. The nineteenth-century background is traced with reference to France and England by Gibson (1989) and Heimann (1995) respectively. Graef (1965) considers the evolution in the cult of the Virgin Mary while Pirotte (1987) provides an excellent case study of the changing images of religious belief. The rich history of pilgrimages and Marian apparitions can be approached through the accounts of Blackbourn (1993), Baumont (1993), Gallagher (1983), Géradin (1947) and Christian (1992 and 1996). Przeciszewski (1988) illustrates the popularity of spiritual movements through the example of Poland while parades and the increasingly visible presence of Catholics in the 'public sphere' are discussed by Fouilloux (1990) and Tranvouez (1983a). The nineteenth-century development of Catholic associations in Germany and the Netherlands is described by Blackbourn (1980) and Wintle (1987). Lijphart (1968), Righart (1986) and Whyte (1981) consider its consequences in terms of a pillarisation of society.

Chadwick (1981) provides a general account of Church–State relations in the early nineteenth century. The subsequent development of conflicts between clericals and anti-clericals in France can be traced in McManners (1972) and Magraw (1983) and in Germany in Sperber (1991) and Sheehan (1978). Riall (1994) discusses Catholicism and Italian nationalism while Wheeler (1978) and Carr (1982) provide accounts of the political struggles between liberals and Catholics in Portugal and Spain. The pontificate of Pius IX is considered in Aubert *et al.* (1981a).

Mayeur (1980) is the only satisfactory general account of Catholic political movements in Europe. The emergence and subsequent development of the Centre Party in Germany is analysed by Anderson (1981), Blackbourn (1980) and Ross (1976). Kossmann (1978) describes events in Belgium and the Netherlands while the slow maturation of Italian Catholic politics is traced in Pollard (1996) and Molony (1977). Altermatt (1979) considers the Swiss KVP, and the Austrian Christian Socials are analysed in considerable detail by Boyer (1981 and 1995). The complex history of Catholic politics in France is summarised in McMillan (1996a). McManners (1972) discusses conflicts of Church and State while insights into French right-wing politics are provided by Sternhell (1978) and Nord (1986). Weber (1962), Cohen (1988) and Barthélemy-Madaule (1973) analyse Action Française and Le Sillon.

A general description of social Catholicism in Europe is presented by Misner (1991). Martin (1978), Poulat (1977) and Mayeur (1972) consider its development and ideology in France; Hilden (1986) and Magraw (1992) provide examples of local Catholic paternalism. The origins of *Rerum Novarum* are analysed in Furlong and Curtis (1994) and placed in the more general context of papal doctrine by Schuck (1991) and Aubert *et al.* (1981b). Patch (1985), Agócs (1988), Neuville (1959) and Conway (1996b) discuss the emergence of working-class Catholic movements. The putative Christian democrat character of pre-1914 social Catholicism is stated emphatically by Fogarty (1957) and criticised from a French perspective by Nord (1984) and Poulat (1975). The significant influence of agrarian lobby groups on Catholic politics is the subject of Farr (1978), Moeller (1986) and Van Molle (1989).

2 The 1920s

Expansion and democratisation

Catholicism was one of the more surprising beneficiaries of the First World War. A war that had been fought in the name of liberal justice and that led to the Bolshevik seizure of power in Russia in 1917 and a series of short-lived socialist revolutions in central Europe in 1918 and 1919 had the more durable consequence of accelerating the emergence of Catholicism as a major force in European political life. The years after the First World War witnessed a rapid broadening of Catholicism as a political force as it spread into many areas of southern and eastern Europe where it had scarcely existed prior to 1914 and as it expanded to include not merely parliamentary and electoral politics but also a wide range of other forms of political action.

The expansion in Catholic politics after the First World War was nowhere more dramatic than in Italy. The Partito Popolare Italiano (Italian People's Party, PPI) held its founding congress in January 1919; later that year the party won 20 per cent of the national vote in the first post-war elections and 100 of its candidates were elected as parliamentary deputies. Together with the Socialists, the Catholics of the PPI became one of the key components of post-war politics in Italy and PPI ministers served in all of the many short-lived coalition governments that ruled Italy from 1919 to 1923. Benefiting from the decision of Pope Benedict XV partially to lift the ban on Catholics participating in the political life of the Italian state, the PPI was the culmination of the gradual development of Catholic politics in northern Italy prior to 1914 and, not surprisingly, its highest levels of electoral support were in those areas of the north-east of the country, notably Lombardy and the Veneto, where it could rely on the support both of the clergy and of the powerful Catholic agricultural syndicates and trade unions.

The PPI was emphatically a Catholic party. Its leader, Don Sturzo, was a Catholic priest and the initial programme of the party issued in

1919 made much of traditional Catholic themes of class collaboration, decentralisation of power and the defence of the family. At the same time, however, the ideology of the PPI reflected the determination of its leaders to forge a party that went beyond the conservative preoccupations of the papacy and of the ecclesiastical hierarchy. The party made little reference to the papacy's unresolved dispute with the Italian state and it received no more than grudging support from the Pope and many of the bishops. Instead, the PPI presented itself as a democratic alternative to liberalism and socialism and, influenced by the new Catholic trade union confederation (the Confederazione Italiana dei Lavoratori, CIL) and its leader Miglioti, it preferred to work with the Socialists in parliament rather than allying itself with the increasingly conservative Liberals.

The remarkable success of the PPI proved, however, to be a transient phenomenon. The party maintained its level of support in the 1921 elections but the rapid rise of Mussolini's Fascist movement had already begun to dominate national and local political life. The PPI failed to build a durable alliance with either the Socialists or the Liberals and, as the political and social crisis deepened, so the more conservative elements in the party began to be drawn toward an alliance with Fascism. The PPI was seeking to occupy a political centre-ground which no longer existed and, after the Fascist March on Rome in October 1922, it agreed to enter a new coalition government led by Mussolini. While the PPI hoped that its presence in the government would act as a restraint on the Fascist leader, subsequent developments rapidly served to demonstrate the weakness of the PPI in the face of Fascist aggrandisement. In the summer of 1923 Sturzo resigned as party leader and in the elections of 1924 a much weakened PPI won only 9 per cent of the vote and many Catholics preferred to support Fascist candidates. Soon afterwards, the rump of beleaguered PPI deputies withdrew from parliament in protest at Fascist violence and, while the papacy sought to build links with the new Fascist regime, the leaders of the PPI were eventually forced to dissolve the party.

The rapid rise and fall of the PPI demonstrated the strengths and weaknesses of political Catholicism, not merely in Italy but also throughout Europe during the 1920s. While its electoral success proved the willingness of the Catholic faithful to vote for and identify with a party that sought not merely to protect Catholic confessional concerns but also to provide a distinctively Catholic solution to the problems of modern Italy, the PPI's subsequent disintegration also highlighted the difficulties of advocating a Catholic political programme that tran-

scended regional and social differences. The PPI was defeated ultimately not only by Fascist violence and by the virtual betrayal of the
party by the papacy but by the divisions that emerged within its own
ranks. The party was always a coalition both of different regional
groups and of divergent social interests and, as politics during the
turbulent post-war years dissolved into bitter local social conflicts, so
the PPI lost much of its coherence. Material concerns took precedence
over loyalty to Catholic principles and, while the Catholic trade unions
sought to protect working-class interests, much of the Catholic bourgeoisie was seduced by Mussolini's rhetoric of law and order.

The PPI was only one of a considerable number of new Catholic
movements which emerged in Europe after the First World War. In the
Netherlands, the Rooms Katholieke Staats Partij (Roman Catholic
State Party, RKSP), founded in 1926, rapidly became a powerful force
in inter-war Dutch politics, while in central and eastern Europe the
demise of the Habsburg and Russian empires created new nation-states
and democratic political systems in which Catholics often constituted
an important presence. Thus, for example, in newly independent
Lithuania it was a Catholic party, the Christian Democrats (Lietuviu
Krikscioniu Demokratu Sajunga), that dominated the Constituent
Assembly and the governments of the early 1920s.

The expansion in Catholic parties evident during the 1920s was not
universal. Two striking exceptions were Poland and Ireland. Both were
new nations which acquired independence after the First World War
and in both cases Catholicism had long been inextricably bound up
with their sense of national identity. Nevertheless, with the exception
of the relatively small Chrzescjanska Demokracja (Christian
Democratic Party) in Poland, in neither country did a Catholic party
of significance emerge. This absence owed much to the power of the
Church hierarchies within the two countries. In both Poland and
Ireland, the bishops intervened actively in political life, in the case of
Ireland by developing close links with both major political forces
(Cumann na nGaedheal and Fianna Fáil) while in Poland the hier-
archy supported Dmowski's Narodowa Demokracja (National
Democrats) against Marshal Pilsudski's more left-wing and in some
respects anti-clerical coalition. Thus, although a vigorous network of
Catholic spiritual and social associations flourished in both countries,
direct political activity remained primarily the concern of the clergy.

Poland and Ireland were not entirely exceptional. In France too the
goal of a single Catholic Party remained illusory. The historical
fissures within the Catholic population, the ambivalence with which
many Catholics still regarded the Third Republic and the traditional

reliance of many Catholics on parties of the conservative right to represent their interests were all factors that hindered the development of an autonomous Catholic politics. Nevertheless, Catholics were an active force in the political life of the inter-war Third Republic. Movements of the right such as Charles Maurras's anti-republican and monarchist *Action Française* appealed directly to Catholic concerns while General de Castelnau's Fédération Nationale Catholique (National Catholic Federation) created in 1924, although it denied that it sought to be a political party, acted in effect as a powerful conservative lobby group in French politics during the subsequent decade. The Fédération represented traditional Catholic views but the 1920s also saw the emergence of an increasingly influential French Christian democrat movement which gave rise notably to the Parti Démocrate Populaire (Democratic Popular Party, PDP). Founded in 1924, the centrist stance of the PDP resembled in many respects the Italian PPI and, while its success was relatively modest (nineteen deputies elected to the Chamber of Deputies in 1928, thirteen in 1936), it did succeed in becoming a voice for those Catholic intellectuals and workers who wished to cast off the legacy of Catholic hostility to the Third Republic.

For a long time, Catholic politics in Spain had been even more emphatically dominated by an antipathy to the values of liberal parliamentarism. Here too, however, the 1920s saw the tentative beginnings of new structures of Catholic political action. As elsewhere in Europe, the new forms of mass politics that developed after the First World War forced Spanish Catholics, almost despite themselves, to contemplate the creation of a party that would defend their interests. The Partido Social Popular (Social Popular Party, PSP) founded by a number of journalists and leaders of social Catholic organisations in 1922 was in effect the first Catholic party in Spain and its leaders made much of their commitment to parliamentary politics. Its basis of support, however, remained meagre. For most Catholics, there remained a fundamental incompatibility between their vision of a monarchist and uniformly Catholic Spain and the model of pluralist politics represented by the PSP. Instead, they rallied to the rhetoric of social order and defence of Catholic values espoused by General Primo de Rivera whose military coup in 1923 brought the brief experiment of the PSP to an abrupt end and inaugurated eight years of authoritarian rule.

This choice between democracy and authoritarianism was also faced by those Catholic parties that had come to prominence before 1914 but which, after the First World War, were confronted by a very different political situation. In Belgium, the introduction of universal manhood suffrage in 1918 destroyed almost at a stroke the Catholic Party's long-standing monopoly over government. Although it emerged as the largest single party in the elections of 1919, it was henceforth obliged to share power with its Liberal and Socialist rivals and throughout the 1920s the party remained bitterly divided between its largely Flemish Christian democrat elements and the anti-democratic attitudes of sections of the francophone bourgeoisie. In Austria, Catholic enthusiasm for the democratic Republic which emerged from the ruins of the Habsburg Empire was always limited. The Christian Social Party rapidly established itself as the dominant party of government in the Republic but, under the leadership of a conservative priest, Ignaz Seipel, its ideology remained firmly rooted in the authoritarian ideas of the past. This was to a large extent the consequence of the revolutionary upheavals of 1918–19 which had followed the collapse of Habsburg power. The bitter legacy of those years cast a long shadow over the politics of the 1920s and ensured that the Republic was always regarded by much of the Catholic popu-lation of provincial Austria as an alien imposition by Viennese revolutionaries. The Christian Social Party exploited this provincial hostility to Vienna. It carefully protected the material interests of its predominantly rural electorate and in many areas of provincial Austria worked closely with the right-wing paramilitary groups, the Heimwehr (Home Guard), which had been founded after the First World War. Consequently, the party's commitment to the rules of democratic poli-tics remained no more than superficial and its bitter rivalry with the Social Democratic Party always threatened to destroy the new Republic.

Nowhere were the political dilemmas confronted by Catholics after the First World War more intense than in Germany. The collapse of the Wilhelmine Empire and the establishment of the democratic Weimar Republic transformed the Zentrumspartei (Centre Party) from being the guardian of the rights of a disadvantaged minority into a central element of the new parliamentary regime. This was a role that the Centre Party was ill equipped to fulfil. The events of the First World War and the subsequent revolutionary upheavals had substantially exacerbated long-standing social and political divisions among German Catholics. Participation in the war effort and the prominent role that Zentrum politicians such as Mathias Erzberger and Adam Stegerwald had played in the foundation of the Weimar Republic encouraged some Catholics to abandon the 'semi-detached' stance towards national politics that had characterised Catholic attitudes during the Wilhelmine Empire.

Especially among the Catholic trade unionists active in the Christian trade union confederation, the Deutscher Gewerkschaftsbund (German Trade Union Federation, DGB) founded in 1919, there was a real enthusiasm to play an active role in the new democratic process which led figures such as Stegerwald to advocate the dissolution of the Centre Party and its replacement by a broadly based non-confessional party of the political centre.

This trend was, however, strenuously opposed by other Catholics for whom the experiences of the war years and the short-lived revolutionary regimes in Berlin and Munich in 1918–19 had strengthened both their confessional identity and their hostility to national politics. Such attitudes were especially prevalent among the Catholic peasant farmers of western and southern Germany, for whom the constraints of the wartime economy and the system of price controls imposed on agricultural products by the early Weimar governments fostered a deep resentment of urban politicians and of democratic politics. Regional differences also came to the fore. In the difficult years after the First World War, local issues seemed more important to many Catholics than national politics. Local peasant defence leagues emerged and in Bavaria the former Centre Party organisations, resentful of the progressive influence of the Catholic trade unions on the national Centre Party leadership, broke away and formed the independent Bayerische Volkspartei (Bavarian People's Party, BVP).

Divided between these divergent elements, the Centre Party struggled to maintain its unity. The bonds of confessional loyalty forged in the struggle against Bismarck's *Kulturkampf* in the 1870s no longer possessed the same emotional force, especially as the constitution of the Weimar Republic, by guaranteeing the legal rights of the Catholic minority, had satisfied many of the party's principal demands. Nevertheless, encouraged by the strenuous efforts of the Church hierarchy to maintain Catholic political unity, the Zentrum survived. Proposals for a deconfessionalisation of the party were decisively rebuffed in 1920 and, under the cautious leadership of the party chairman Wilhelm Marx, the party participated in all of the many coalition governments of the 1920s. The bonds of party unity did, however, remain tenuous. Fearful of exacerbating divisions between its right and left wings, the Zentrum avoided making a clear statement of support for the democratic structures of the Weimar Republic and regional differences remained marked. In Prussia, for example, the Centre Party collaborated closely with the left-wing Social Democrats, while in predominantly rural areas such as the Palatinate Catholic peasant farmers remained alienated from the Weimar political system.

The difficulties experienced by the Centre Party contrasted markedly with the vitality of other aspects of German Catholic life during the Weimar Republic. Catholics constituted 32.5 per cent of the population in 1930 and they remained for the most part strongly conscious of their distinct identity. Levels of religious practice were high and there was a substantial and flourishing network of confessional social and cultural associations. But the notion of a single party representative of the distinct political interests of the Catholic minority no longer reflected the reality of a more fractured Catholic population. Thus, although the enfranchisement of women initially gave a boost to the Centre Party's share of the vote, it fell back steadily during the 1920s. In 1919, 62.8 per cent of Catholics voted for the Centre Party; by 1930 the figure was only 47 per cent. For the first time since the 1870s, the Centre Party enjoyed the support of only a minority of German Catholics and during the 1920s Catholics were active in a number of other parties, including the Social Democrats and the right-wing Deutschnationale Volkspartei (German National People's Party, DNVP).

The very different forms of Catholic political activity in Germany, France and Italy during the 1920s demonstrated the extent to which patterns of Catholic politics were determined by the influence of particular national circumstances. Nevertheless, they also had a number of factors in common. Foremost among these was undoubtedly the impact of the First World War. In all areas of Catholic Europe, with the partial exception of the Iberian peninsula, Catholic politics was dominated during the 1920s by the legacy of that conflict. Its profound consequences and, more especially, the traumatic impact of the war on the lives of millions of Europeans could not fail to have a substantial impact on Catholicism. In religious terms, the manifold uncertainties and sufferings of the war provoked a rise in the intensity of religious practice. Not merely at the front line but also among the civilian populations, there was a return to Catholicism as people sought solace and reassurance in the structures of religious faith. Shrines constructed in the trenches of the Western Front, the distribution of images of saints or of the Sacred Heart and, above all, the wave of appeals to the Virgin Mary were all facets of this surge in popular religiosity which, although it was often crudely focused on pleas for self-preservation or the safe return of loved ones, was not without a more lasting significance. The war reversed the marginalisation of religion which had taken place during the late nineteenth century and, although the wartime rises in church attendance often fell away rapidly once peace returned, the experiences of the war years contributed to the new-found vitality of the Catholic faith during the 1920s.

The war also had more tangible benefits for the Church. In France, it brought Church and State together in a *union sacrée* (sacred union) against the German enemy and enabled a compromise to be found which defused the long-standing conflict between the Church and the Third Republic. More generally, conflicts between clericals and anticlericals ceased to exert their former considerable influence over the terms of political debate. Although the power of the Church remained a major political issue in Spain and Portugal, elsewhere in Europe liberal and socialist antipathy to Catholicism became more muted during the inter-war years. Rationalism and militant atheism were no longer fashionable (except on the extreme left), and among certain intellectuals – especially in France – Catholic ideas enjoyed a revival during the 1920s.

If the First World War had in some respects created a more favourable situation for the Catholic religion, it also presented Catholic political movements with new challenges. In particular, the war accelerated the transition to an era of mass politics. The extent of this change varied in different regions of Europe. In states such as France and Germany, as well as in many of the major cities of Europe, structures of mass politics were already well developed by 1900 but, in central and southern Europe as well as in many rural areas, the changes brought about by the First World War were much more dramatic. As the revolutionary upheavals during 1919 and 1920 vividly demonstrated, former structures of clientelism and paternalistic rule had been replaced by a new world in which power depended on the ability to rally popular support. The establishment of new parliamentary constitutions in Germany and the former Habsburg territories, as well as the democratic suffrage reforms elsewhere in Europe, reinforced this change of political culture. Popular movements, election campaigns and mass demonstrations were the new tools of politics and, although Mussolini's seizure of power in Italy and Primo de Rivera's coup in Spain soon demonstrated that they could also be used to oppose democratic politics, all political forces were obliged to accept their importance.

The establishment of new Catholic parties such as the PPI in Italy reflected this ascendancy of mass politics. Although they built on the examples of the pre-1914 parties, the Catholic movements of the inter-war years were much more directly oriented towards winning the support of their electorate. As the difficulties of the Centre Party in Germany well illustrated, it was, on the whole, no longer sufficient for Catholic parties to rely on appeals to confessional solidarity and the directives of priests to win elections. The support of Catholic electors could not be taken for granted; it had to be earned and maintained. This change was especially evident in rural areas where requisitioning and taxation policies during the First World War had radicalised farmers and made them very conscious of the need to protect their economic interests against the priorities of the predominantly urban political elites. A strong undercurrent of urban–rural tension ran through many facets of the history of Europe during the 1920s and 1930s but the problems that this presented for Catholic parties were especially acute. Often heavily reliant on the support of rural electors, Catholic parties had to try to balance the defence of the farming community against the demands of their working-class and bourgeois supporters.

The democratisation of politics evident in much of Europe after the First World War was, thus, also a force that made itself felt within the structures of political Catholicism. This was especially so in the case of the Catholic working class. The immediate post-war years witnessed a dramatic expansion in Catholic trade unionism. In 1919, in addition to the foundation of the Christian trade union grouping, the DGB, in Germany, new Catholic trade union confederations were created in France (the Confédération Française du Travail Catholique, CFTC) and Italy (the Confederazione Italiana dei Lavoratori, CIL). Together with similar initiatives in a number of other countries, these move-ments established working-class trade unions as a significant force in Catholic politics. Certainly, their development was often slow. In Spain, efforts to found a Catholic trade union independent of clerical control foundered after the First World War and in most countries membership of Catholic unions remained relatively small in compar-ison with the well-established Socialist unions. Nevertheless, membership of the Catholic trade unions increased rapidly during the 1920s, rising, for example, in Belgium from 133,156 in 1925 to 304,010 in 1933.

These Catholic trade unions were the culmination of the gradual development in Catholic workers' organisations since the 1890s and marked a coming of age of Catholic working-class action. While the pre-war movements had often operated under clerical or middle-class direction, those of the 1920s were emphatically controlled by workers and frequently came into conflict with the ecclesiastical hierarchy and with the Catholic political parties. They were also increasingly willing to intervene directly in the political process. Throughout the 1920s, Stegerwald's DGB was a powerful lobby group both within and outside the Centre Party, while in the Netherlands the so-called 'Michaelists', a grouping of Catholic working-class organisations, sought to influence the direction of the Catholic Party, the RKSP. Similarly in Belgium Catholic working-class groups were an increasingly self-assertive presence within the Catholic Party and in 1925 encouraged the left wing of the party to go into coalition with the Socialists despite the fierce opposition of its bourgeois leadership.

Trade unions formed one element of a network of Catholic working-class organisations which also encompassed insurance leagues, co-operatives and youth organisations such as the Jeunesse Ouvrière Chrétienne (Christian Workers' Youth, JOC). Founded in 1925 by a Belgian priest, Joseph Cardijn, the JOC rapidly developed both in Belgium and in France, where for its tenth anniversary in 1937, 80,000 'Jocists' attended a rally in Paris. Strongly influenced by the militant Catholic Action rhetoric of the time, the JOC saw itself as a spiritual movement of the Catholic laity devoted to the rechristianisation of the working class. It shunned direct political engagement but through its wide range of social and cultural activities it played a decisive role in training a new generation of Catholic working-class leaders. It was those industrial regions where Catholics constituted a significant element of the population such as the Nord in France, the Ruhr in Germany and Upper Silesia in Poland that constituted the bastions of these working-class Catholic organisations. Aided by sympathetic clerics, such as Cardinal Liénart who was appointed Bishop of Lille in 1928, they formed a self-contained Catholic world composed of its own organisations, press and mentality.

The term 'Christian democrat' was widely used by both Catholic working-class militants and their opponents to describe the political outlook of this milieu. In so far as this label reflected their commitment to working within democratic political structures to achieve their goals, it was an accurate description. Much more so than the social Catholic movements of the pre-1914 years, the Catholic working-class groups of the 1920s combined their ambition for a more just society with a commitment to democratic political structures. The nostalgia for a pre-industrial *ancien régime*, evident in social Catholic groups at the turn of the century, had been swept away by the First World War. Nevertheless, it would be wrong to exaggerate the similarities between these organisations and the Christian Democrat parties established in much of western Europe after the Second World War. While the latter were largely middle class in their leadership and presented themselves as the voice of Christian ideas within a predominantly secular and pluralist society, the working-class movements of the inter-war years remained loyal to a more traditional definition of Catholic political action. Certainly some intellectuals, such as those associated with the newspaper *L'Aube* (Dawn) in France in the 1930s, advocated ideas that pre-figured the Christian democrat ideology of the post-1945 era; but they remained a small minority. Most Catholic working-class groups did not favour such ideas. Instead, they saw themselves as the representatives of the confessional interests of Catholicism within the working class and, though often willing to collaborate with Socialist and other non-Catholic groups to achieve specific goals, they remained convinced that only the establishment of a society based on Catholic principles offered a durable solution to the sufferings of the working class.

The internal democratisation of Catholic politics represented by the expansion in Catholic working-class organisations was not the only force working to change Catholicism from within. A second important factor was the spiritual revival which affected much of Catholic Europe during the 1920s. Reflected in increased participation in pilgrimages, religious retreats and in the mass membership of Catholic spiritual associations such as the various Catholic Action organisations, this upsurge in religious commitment had both long-term and short-term origins. As we have seen, the new-found willingness of many Catholics to place their religious faith at the centre of their lives formed part of a longer evolution in the nature of religious practice from social convention to personal belief. It also reflected, however, the impact of specific institutional and social trends. In particular, the new mood of religious militancy during the 1920s owed much to the increased importance of the papacy and of a younger Catholic intelligentsia within Catholicism after the First World War.

During the pontificate of Pius XI from 1922 to 1939, the papacy acquired an unprecedented centrality in Catholic life. Pius was not content merely to exercise a moral authority over the life of the Church; he wished to be its ruler. Building on the measures initiated by his predecessors, he therefore strengthened the Vatican bureaucracy, the *curia*, established his authority over the religious orders and ensured that key appointments of bishops were brought under his direct control. These organisational changes were intended to serve a clear spiritual purpose. Pius XI was determined to liberate the Church from the defensive priorities of the nineteenth century and to transform it into an apostolic organisation committed to the rechristianisation of modern society. Thus, he had little interest in those forms of Catholic political action that he believed distracted the faithful from this spiritual goal, and he watched with indifference the Fascist offensive against the PPI as well as intervening in December 1926 to issue a condemnation of the nationalist *Action Française* movement of Charles Maurras which had long enjoyed considerable support among conservative French Catholics.

Instead of depending on parties to protect Catholic interests, Pius XI preferred to sign diplomatic concordats with national governments which, by guaranteeing the legal independence of the Catholic Church from state control, provided the freedom for its spiritual and cultural organisations to pursue their apostolic work. Forty such concordats were concluded by the Vatican during the inter-war years, including those with Poland in 1925, with Mussolini's Italy in 1929 (the so-called Lateran Treaties) and, most controversially, with Nazi Germany in 1933. The treaties were intended primarily to serve the second element of Pius XI's programme: the establishment of movements of Catholic Action. These were the central agents of Pius XI's vision for the Church. As expressed in his inaugural encyclical *Ubi Arcano Dei* in 1922 and reiterated in many of his subsequent public statements, Catholic Action groups were the means of 'the organised participation of the laity in the hierarchical apostolate of the Church, transcending party politics for the establishment of Christ's reign throughout the world'. During the 1920s, the Vatican therefore encouraged the formation of movements of Catholic Action in all of the principal states of Catholic Europe, even intervening directly, as in the case of Germany, to overcome the hesitations of the national bishops.

Aided by this explicit papal support, Catholic Action movements soon emerged as a highly visible presence in Catholic life. The demonstrations, parades and rallies of Catholic Action aped the structures of modern mass politics and consciously sought to reassert the public prominence of the Catholic faith. Their strength varied, but in many countries – most especially in France, Belgium, Poland, Hungary and Italy – they became substantial mass movements which mobilised large numbers of the Catholic faithful in support of their campaigns. All sections of the laity were involved. Not surprisingly, however, their strength was greatest among the young, for whom subsidiary organisations for students and young farmers and workers were created. The membership of Catholic Action groups ran into many thousands and, although clearly not all of these members shared the attitudes of their leaders, it is evident that their activism and militant rhetoric did hold a real appeal for the more committed laity that had emerged in much of Europe.

The goals of Catholic Action groups were never clearly defined. They remained aloof from party politics and concentrated instead on spiritual and social issues, such as campaigns against pornography, proselytisation among the dechristianised working classes and glorifications of the virtues of motherhood, youth and the family. The more general character of Catholic Action movements was, however, heavily influenced by the new and more radical tone of Catholic propaganda initiated by Pius XI. It was the vision of the Church militant, imposing its values on a decadent and materialist society, that predominated in Catholic Action rhetoric and was often accompanied by utopian dreams of a 'rechristianisation' of society. This quasi-revivalist rhetoric found its clearest expression in the prominence given by Catholic Action groups to the cult of Christ the King reigning in majesty over the world. In many ways the opposite of the more personal and introverted Marian symbolism of late nineteenth-century Catholicism, this vision of the rule of Christ and – by extension – of Christian values was a largely novel feature of Catholicism during the inter-war years and received direct encouragement from Pius XI in his encyclical *Quas Primas* of 1925.

The rapid success of Catholic Action movements was a product both of papal encouragement and of the energy and commitment of a younger Catholic intelligentsia. The emergence of a new generation of educated Catholics eager to devote themselves to their faith was one of the most important developments within Catholicism during the 1920s. It was not without precedents. Already in the years before 1914, intellectual groups and periodicals had become an increasingly prominent feature of Catholic life in a number of countries such as France; but it was indisputably after the First World War that this Catholic intelligentsia came to the fore as an influential force among the Catholic laity. This process owed much to changes in education. Since the late nineteenth century, the Church had sought, wherever possible, to develop its own structures of Catholic secondary and higher education independent of the secular power of the state. The importance of these Catholic educational systems varied greatly between different countries but the unprecedented Catholic investment in education had the consequence of creating a more educated and self-confident youth, conscious of their Catholic identity and confident in their intellectual beliefs.

It was the Catholic universities of Europe that were the central focus of this new Catholic intelligentsia. Although access to university remained limited to a privileged few, the numbers of students rose steadily in most countries during the 1920s, reflecting the increased willingness of the bourgeoisie to invest in the professional education of their children. Catholic universities such as Coimbra in Portugal, Louvain in Belgium, Nijmegen in the Netherlands, Lublin in Poland and Kaunas in Lithuania became centres of a vigorous Catholic intellectual culture which was reflected in a plethora of student movements and periodicals. The 1920s and 1930s were a golden age for Catholic intellectual journals and revues which, although their circulation was relatively small, often had considerable influence in terms of distributing and popularising the ideas of the Catholic intellectual elite.

This Catholic student culture was strongly marked by the more militant style of Catholicism evident in Catholic Action movements. Its heroes were figures such as the nineteenth-century French writer Léon Bloy or, in the 1930s, the theologian and philosopher Jacques Maritain whose writings asserted the autonomy and distinctiveness of Catholic beliefs. This 'exclusivist' mentality also encouraged dreams of a Catholic reorganisation of society. The wider trend in much of post-war intellectual life away from liberal positivism towards a renewed interest in mysticism and the irrational, as well as the influence among Catholic intellectuals of neo-Thomist theology which drew its inspiration from the thirteenth-century writings of St Thomas Aquinas, encouraged the Catholic intelligentsia to think of Catholicism as providing a comprehensive answer to the problems of contemporary society. Confronted by the apparent demise of an old intellectual and political world in the barbarism of the First World War, Catholic intellectuals of the 1920s repeatedly insisted that, by reconciling the interests of the individual and the community, Catholic social and political ideas offered salvation for a European civilisation torn between the twin evils of liberal individualism and Marxist collectivism.

The political consequences of the more radical Catholic mood evident in Catholic Action movements and student circles were ambivalent. By encouraging the faithful to place Catholicism at the centre of their lives, it undoubtedly helped to consolidate the interconnection between religious belief and political choices and action. In other respects, however, the spiritual campaigns of the 1920s distanced Catholics from the political process. As parties such as the German Centre Party and the Belgian Catholic Party discovered to their cost, the new Catholic Action groups drew many younger Catholics away from active involvement in politics and there was a marked decline in the membership and activism of the youth movements of Catholic parties in a number of countries during the 1920s. More importantly, the new priorities espoused by Catholic Action groups and by the papacy accorded greater importance to spiritual and proselytising campaigns than to political action. The primarily defensive priorities of the pre-1914 Catholic parties no longer accorded with the more militant and triumphalist rhetoric of post-war Catholicism and, especially in the eyes of some younger intellectuals, even the notion of a Catholic party protecting the Church and the faithful appeared to be the outmoded legacy of a past era. A distaste for the manoeuvrings and compromises of parliamentary politics was evident among many younger Catholic militants during the 1920s and, rather than acting within the structures of the liberal political system, Catholicism, so these radicals argued, should seek to bring about a wide-ranging transformation of contemporary society by restoring the centrality of Catholic teachings and morality.

The legacy of the 1920s for Catholic political action was, thus, a complex one. If the democratic reforms and revolutionary upheavals of the immediate post-war years had stimulated a surge in Catholic political engagement, the manifold changes wrought (or accelerated) by the First World War had also in many respects undermined the social and intellectual assumptions that had governed pre-1914 Catholic political action. The internal democratisation of Catholic politics had liberated Catholic workers from deference to bourgeois and clerical leaders and had forged Christian democrat movements which co-existed uneasily with the middle-class and rural electorates within the established Catholic parties. In addition, the quasi-revivalist atmosphere evident among many younger Catholics during the 1920s, and which found expression in the success enjoyed by Catholic Action groups, had created a more volatile mood among the Catholic laity in which reliance upon political parties to defend the interests of the faith no longer seemed either natural or desirable. Thus, although the 1920s was a decade of expansion and innovation in forms of Catholic political engagement, it was also a period of divergence and, to some extent, of fragmentation. By the end of the decade, Catholics were a more vocal and visible presence in European political life, but they were also indisputably less united.

BIBLIOGRAPHICAL NOTES

General accounts of the PPI include those of Molony (1977), Webster (1960) and Pollard (1996). Morgan (1995) and Lyttelton (1987) situate the party in the context of Italy's post-war crisis. Kelikian (1986) and Cardoza (1982), among others, illustrate its regional diversity. Beaufays (1973) and Luykx (1996) analyse Catholic politics in the Netherlands while Vardys (1965) and Von Rauch (1974) describe those in Lithuania. The Irish and Polish 'exceptions' can be explored through Lee (1989) and Keogh (1986) for Ireland and Polonsky (1972) and Pease (1991) for Poland. McMillan (1996a) and Paxton (1987) serve as introductions to French Catholic politics. McMillan (1996b) considers de Castelnau's Fédération and Delbreil (1990) provides a comprehensive account of the PDP. Becker (1994) and Chaline (1993) analyse the broader changes to French Catholicism wrought by the First World War. Paul (1967) discusses relations between the Church and the Republic. Events in Spain are described in Vincent (1996a) and Ben-Ami (1983).

Changes in established Catholic parties are described with reference to Belgium in Gerard (1985) and Conway (1996b) and with reference to Austria in Von Klemperer (1972), Carsten (1977), Diamant (1960) and Jeffery (1995). Evans (1981) and Lönne (1996) provide general accounts of the German Centre Party during the Weimar Republic and their evidence of the party's internal divisions is amply confirmed by the comprehensive biography of Wilhelm Marx by Von Hehl (1987). The party's progressive wing is the subject of Patch (1985) and Kohler (1990) while the depth of Catholic rural bitterness towards Weimar is highlighted by Moeller (1986) and Osmond (1993). Schönhoven (1977) analyses the rightward drift of the BVP.

The surge in Catholic trade unions and workers' organisations has stimulated a substantial literature. In addition to the works already mentioned by Patch (1985) (Germany), Morgan (1995) (Italy) and Conway (1996b) (Belgium), Pierrard (1984) and Launay (1986) analyse developments in France and Callahan (1995) discusses the 'failure' of Catholic trade unionism in Spain. Arnal (1987) and the collective volume on *Cardijn* (1983) trace the expansion of the JOC. Mayeur (1966) provides a history of *L'Aube*. Masson-Gadenne (1991) and Polonsky (1972) illustrate the Catholic working-class cultures of the Nord and Upper Silesia.

Pius XI's ambitions for Catholicism are analysed in the fine study by Agostino (1991). Holmes (1981) and Rhodes (1973) provide more general descriptions of the policies of the papacy. Pollard (1985) is an excellent study of the Church's dealings with the Italian Fascist regime, while Arnal (1985) traces the attitude of the Church towards Action Française. The papal concordat policy is outlined in Conway (1996a) and considered in detail in Stehlin (1983 and 1994). Agostino (1991) and Holmes (1981) demonstrate the papal impulse behind Catholic Action movements while their development in different countries can be explored through Fouilloux (1992a), Chélini (1983), Pollard (1985), De Grazia (1992), Gergely (1977) and Conway (1990). The new-found importance of universities and periodicals in Catholic intellectual life is displayed by Gallagher (1996), Vardys (1978), Przeciszewski (1988) and Winock (1975). Evans (1981) and Gerard (1985) illustrate the alienation of young militants from established Catholic parties.

3 The 1930s

Radicalisation and authoritarianism

The 1930s was a decade of unprecedented flux in Catholic political fortunes. Moments of almost utopian optimism alternated with darker periods of oppression and suffering. While some movements strove to implement radical programmes of Catholic-inspired political and economic reform, others were obliged to defend the Church and faithful against persecution by hostile regimes and movements. Above all, however, the pattern of Catholic politics was determined by three successive but closely inter-related events: the world economic depression, the emergence of the fascist extreme right and the Spanish Civil War. All were events that posed particular difficulties for Catholic political movements. The Depression had an especial impact upon Catholic parties, many of whose traditional supporters – the peasant farmers and the middle classes – suffered disproportionately from its consequences. The rise of fascist movements in Germany and a number of other European states during the 1930s did not merely challenge the electoral base of Catholic parties but their ambition to bring all areas of national life under the control of the state also directly threatened the autonomy of the Church and of Catholic social organisations. Finally, the Spanish Civil War and the wider diplomatic and political conflict that it seemed to presage presented Catholics in Spain and elsewhere in Europe with an awkward dilemma between support for the legitimate (but also anti-clerical) Republic and support for General Franco's Nationalist forces who loudly proclaimed their loyalty to the Catholic Church but who were increasingly reliant upon German and Italian military aid.

Confronted by these challenges, it was scarcely surprising that the 1930s should also have witnessed considerable changes and innovations within Catholic political ranks. Many of the established parties which, since the late nineteenth century, had been the principal agents of Catholic political action were forcibly dissolved or were superseded by new movements less rooted in parliamentary politics and frequently more militant in their rhetoric and ideology. Consequently, the change in Catholic politics in the 1930s was not merely one of personnel and of structures but also, above all, one of mentality. A new openness to alliances with non-Catholic forces of the left and right was one symptom of this change, but so too was an increased confidence that Catholicism alone offered a solution to the manifold problems facing Europe. The radicalism evident in much of Catholic politics during the 1930s undoubtedly reflected the harsh conflicts of the era; but it was also the expression of the more militant mentality of many Catholics who saw the goal of their political action as the achievement of a new social and political order based on Catholic principles.

The unprecedented economic Depression, which spread so rapidly and with such devastating effect over Europe following the Wall Street Crash of 1929, ripped apart the social and political compromises upon which the established Catholic parties had been based. The Centre Party in Germany, the Catholic Party in Belgium and the Christian Social Party in Austria, among others, were all undermined by the rapid fall in living standards and often bitter social conflicts that the Depression provoked. The ascendancy of confessional loyalties over those of class which these parties exemplified was not so much destroyed as submerged by the socio-economic tensions of the era. As the Depression remorselessly deepened during the early 1930s, Catholic unity throughout Europe gave way to the defence of conflicting sectional interests. Catholic farmers, radicalised by the impact of the substantial decline in prices for many of their products on an already fragile agricultural sector, demanded protectionism and price-support measures while, conversely, Catholic workers' organisations demanded cheap food and state welfare programmes to help the urban unemployed. Civil servants sought to protect their salaries against the policies of financial retrenchment followed by most European governments while shopkeepers and members of professions demanded lower taxes and an end to government regulation.

The tensions imposed on Catholic political unity by the Depression were greatest in those countries where Catholics participated in government. In Belgium, the Catholic Party retained governmental power throughout the 1930s but it was weakened both by Christian democrat attacks on the deflationary policies of the Catholic-led governments and by the defection of a considerable proportion of the party's rural and middle-class votes to the forces of the extreme right represented by the Flemish Nationalists and Rexists. In Austria, the demise of the Christian Social Party was much more dramatic.

Deprived of its long-standing leader, Ignaz Seipel, who resigned as chancellor in 1929 and as party leader in 1930, the Christian Socials were overwhelmed by the surge in support among their predominantly rural and provincial electorate for the extra-parliamentary authoritarian right represented by the Heimwehr patriotic leagues. Though riven by internal divisions and weak leadership, the Heimwehr's militant rhetoric of defence of the values (and material interests) of rural, Catholic Austria was much more in tune with the mood of the times and, as political conflict with the Social Democrats descended into virtual civil war, so the Christian Socials were remorselessly forced into dependence on the forces of the extra-parliamentary right. In May 1932 a former minister of agriculture, Engelbert Dollfuss, became chancellor at the head of a coalition government of Heimwehr representatives, peasant defence leagues and the Christian Socials. Dollfuss had little time either for the Republic or for the parliamentary conservatism that the Christian Social Party incarnated. In March 1933, he dismissed parliament, reorganised his government to minimise party political influence and, after violently crushing the Social Democratic militias in Vienna in February 1934, declared a new authoritarian constitution on 1 May 1934.

It was, however, in Germany that the political consequences of the Depression proved to be the most far reaching. The demise of the democratic institutions of the Weimar Republic and the Nazi acquisition of power in January 1933 exemplified the traumatic impact of the Depression on European political structures. As a major party of the democratic middle ground and the traditional representative of the Catholic minority of the population, the Zentrumspartei (Centre Party) ought to have been one of the pillars of the Weimar political system. Its representatives remained in government during most of the final years of the Republic and, compared with the rapid disintegration of the parties of the centre right, it retained much of its electoral support. But the unity of the Centre Party was in many respects more apparent than real. The crisis of the late 1920s and early 1930s exacerbated the regional and social tensions long present within its ranks and largely prevented the Zentrum from playing a decisive political role. In 1928, the conciliatory party president, Wilhelm Marx, retired and he was replaced by Ludwig Kaas, a priest and a representative of the party's conservative wing. Kaas accelerated the evolution of the party towards the political right which had been evident since the mid-1920s. Catholic workers' organisations, notably the Christian trade union confederation, the DGB, lost much of their former influence and the party distanced itself from support for the Republic in favour of echoing the populist and often anti-democratic rhetoric of many of its middle-class and rural supporters.

The rightward shift by the Centre Party was contemporary with but separate from the emergence of Nazism as a major political force. Catholic attitudes towards the Nazi Party (Nationalsozialistische Deutsche Arbeiterpartei, NSDAP) prior to 1933 were largely (though certainly not universally) hostile. Whatever their increasing dissatisfaction with the Weimar Republic, most German Catholics tended to follow their ecclesiastical leaders in regarding Hitler and his followers as a threat to Catholic interests and values. This distrust was largely historical in origin. Nazi racial ideology might indeed have contradicted Christian teachings but of greater importance for most Catholics was the fact that the aggressive nationalism of the Nazis and their glorification of a secular German state appeared to many Catholics to herald a return to the centralised Bismarckian Reich and its oppression of the rights of the Catholic minority. Regional and confessional identities therefore reinforced themselves in encouraging the Catholic populations of southern and western Germany to remain aloof from Nazism. Catholic social organisations, such as trade unions and student organisations, condemned Nazi policies and Catholics were under-represented among the membership of the NSDAP. Catholics also tended not to vote for the party. If one definitive conclusion has emerged from the great wealth of statistical research that has been conducted in recent years on the electoral basis of Nazism, it is that the higher the proportion of Catholics in an electoral district, the lower tended to be the level of support for the NSDAP. There were, however, prominent exceptions. Especially in some rural areas, such as the Palatinate and the Black Forest, Catholics did vote in significant numbers for the NSDAP. Here, economic desperation and a bitter hostility to the perceived urban priorities of the Weimar governments were sufficient to push Catholic peasant farmers into support for Nazism.

If a majority of German Catholics did not vote for Nazism, their commitment to the democratic structures of the Weimar Republic nevertheless waned considerably during the political and economic crisis of the early 1930s. In March 1930, an economist, Heinrich Brüning, became German chancellor and formed a government which ruled by executive decree. Brüning was a Catholic and no supporter of Nazism but his willingness to bypass parliament in effect marked a rejection of the spirit, if not of the letter, of the Weimar constitution. The Centre Party largely supported Brüning but the deflationary policies of his government merely served to exacerbate the political and economic divisions within Catholic ranks. New elections in July 1932 brought further substantial gains for the Nazis and, during the subsequent six months of complex manoeuvring which culminated eventually in Hitler's appointment as chancellor in January 1933, Catholic leaders proved unable to act as a united political force. While the left of the Centre Party, led by Stegerwald of the DGB, still advocated a republican coalition with the Socialists, others were willing to work with Nazism. The Bavarian Catholic party, the BVP, openly supported such a 'Brown–Black' alliance which was also increasingly favoured by small-business and farmers' groupings within the Zentrum. The leading figure of this Catholic right was Franz von Papen. He had long been popular with Catholic agricultural organisations and had broken with the Centre Party in the summer of 1932 in order to forge a short-lived right-wing coalition government. During the final months of 1932 von Papen played a major role in advocating a Nazi-led coalition government, and when Hitler took office in January 1933 von Papen was appointed as his vice-chancellor.

Thus, if the direct responsibility of German Catholics for the success of Nazism was relatively limited, their indirect contribution to the end of the Weimar Republic and the subsequent transition to Nazi rule cannot be denied. Catholics might not have proved as susceptible as their compatriots to Nazi electoral demagogy but they had shared in the general dissatisfaction with the Weimar political system and, although retrospective judgements are all too easy, many Catholic leaders (though certainly not all of them) contributed to the process that led to the Nazi acquisition of power. This ambivalent attitude remained evident during the consolidation of the new regime after January 1933. The Centre Party was not part of the Hitler–von Papen government and in the final elections of 5 March 1933 the party managed – despite the general air of Nazi intimidation which surrounded the election campaign – to win 11.2 per cent of the vote (compared with 11.9 per cent in the previous elections in November 1932). This remarkable achievement demonstrated well the determination of many German Catholics to retain their political autonomy but it proved to be only a temporary obstacle to Hitler's ambitions. Despite ample evidence of the determination of the Nazis to monopolise power in their own hands and to dismantle all other political organisations, the newly elected Centre Party deputies in the Reichstag voted on 23 March for the Enabling Law which granted Hitler extensive powers to circumvent parliament. This fateful act, which led rapidly to the enforced dissolution of the Centre Party, was taken amidst an atmosphere heavy with political and physical intimidation but it marked in effect a decision by the Catholic political and ecclesiastical leadership to sacrifice political autonomy in favour of reaching an accommodation with the Nazi regime. The Zentrum leaders had received largely worthless assurances from Hitler prior to the vote on the Enabling Act regarding the protection of Catholic confessional organisations, and a few days later the German Catholic bishops issued a public statement on 28 March which abandoned their former condemnations of National Socialism in favour of expressing their willingness to work with the Nazi government. Finally, in July 1933, the papacy added its own support to this conciliatory stance by signing a wide-ranging concordat with Hitler.

The rightward evolution in Catholic loyalties evident in Germany during the final years of the Weimar Republic was repeated in much of the rest of Europe during the early 1930s. The impact of the economic depression and the consequent renewed fears of revolutionary upheaval combined to draw most Catholic political movements remorselessly towards the right. The trend was certainly not universal. For some trade unions and workers' organisations, the experience of the Depression led them to find unprecedented common ground with their Socialist rivals. But these Christian democrat groups formed an increasingly beleaguered minority within Catholic political ranks. Instead, their predominantly rural and middle-class composition, as well as the Catholic intellectual culture of the era, encouraged many Catholic movements to abandon their predominantly centrist political stance in favour of the anti-parliamentary slogans and authoritarian ideas of the right. The centre of gravity of political Catholicism had emphatically moved to the right and hostility to the pluralist principles of democratic politics, support for the replacement of directly elected parliaments by a structure of socio-economic corporations and a strong anti-communism were all prominent features of the rhetoric and policies of Catholic movements during the 1930s.

The rapprochement with the right was a product of the radicalisation of much of the Catholic electorate and of the emergence of a new generation of younger political leaders who had been forged in the spiritual movements of the 1920s. Often former militants of Catholic Action groups, they were much less inclined than their elders to accept the compromises and coalitions of parliamentary politics and demanded the introduction of wide-ranging political and social reforms based on Catholic principles. This interconnection between the spiritual crusades of the 1920s and the more radical Catholic politics of the 1930s is central to an understanding of the militant tone that suffused many Catholic political movements of the era. The defence of sectional economic interests, populist denunciations of the failings of the democratic elites and dreams of a Catholic reconquest of the atheist modern world combined to produce a radical and, on occasions, almost millenarian rhetoric which emphatically rejected the cautious and predominantly defensive priorities of the Catholic movements of the past.

Periodicals and student organisations played a prominent part in this new Catholic politics. In France, for example, a number of new groupings emerged during the early 1930s, often based around periodicals published by young intellectuals. Some of these periodicals such as *Sept* (Seven) or *L'Aube* were associated with the Christian democratic tradition of Marc Sangnier and of the Parti Démocrate Populaire. But many of them, such as *Esprit* (Spirit) founded by Emmanuel Mounier and a group of like-minded friends in 1932, were strongly influenced by the anti-parliamentary ideas fashionable at the time. Although it claimed to reject conventional political divisions and spoke grandiloquently of how Catholicism offered a 'third way' (*une troisième voie*) between liberalism and fascism, *Esprit* shared the widespread conviction of those on the French right that the parliamentary parties and short-lived coalition governments of the Third Republic should be replaced by a new political structure. Thus, although Mounier and his colleagues can certainly not be described with much plausibility as 'fascists', their calls for a new political and social order inspired by Catholic values reflected the similarities that existed between the goals of these young Catholic militants and those of the various leagues and parties of the French anti-republican right.

The principal characteristics of *Esprit* – namely a radical Catholic rhetoric combined with opposition to liberal political and social principles – were evident among many Catholic movements elsewhere in Europe. In Belgium, both some Flemish nationalist groups and the predominantly francophone Christus Rex (Christ the King) movement, founded by students and intellectuals at the University of Louvain, reflected the influence of these anti-democratic ideas. This was especially so of Rex, which, under the demagogic leadership of Léon Degrelle, transformed itself into a political party and, by combining militant Catholic rhetoric with populist denunciations of the failings of the democratic parties, succeeded in winning 11.5 per cent of the vote in the elections of 1936.

Similar ideas were also popular among many younger Dutch Catholics during the 1930s, notably those active in the Gemeenschap (Community) movement of Anton Van Duinkerken, and in Ireland, where Catholic corporatist and authoritarian ideas exerted considerable influence over the Blueshirt movement. This uniformed organisation (the formal title of which was the National Guard) had been founded by elements opposed to the Fianna Fáil government led by Éamon de Valera which had come to power after the elections of February 1932. Its leader was General Eoin O'Duffy, who was sacked in 1933 as the Irish police commissioner by de Valera, and the movement drew its strength from the deep antagonism forged during the Civil War of the early 1920s between the intransigent nationalist tradition represented by Fianna Fáil and the more flexible stance of William T. Cosgrave's Cumann na nGaedheal party. The latter had ruled the Irish Free State since it acquired *de facto* independence from Britain in the treaty of 1921 and close links existed between Cosgrave's government and the hierarchy of the Catholic Church. The electoral defeat of Cumann na nGaedheal in 1932 sidelined its moderate parliamentary leadership, opening the way to O'Duffy and to a younger generation of radicals influenced by European Catholic ideas. A new movement, Fine Gael, was founded in August 1933 out of the fusion of Cumann na nGaedheal and the Blueshirts, and O'Duffy was elected as its president. He proved, however, to be an impulsive leader. After an abortive Blueshirt march in Dublin in August 1933, modelled on Mussolini's March on Rome, he was implicated in various violent incidents enabling Cosgrave to regain control of Fine Gael in 1934 and reassert a more cautious political strategy.

Catholic anti-democratic ideas remained a vocal force in Irish political life during the 1930s. The social Catholic doctrines espoused by the papacy in *Quadragesimo Anno* had a particular impact in Ireland, and in August 1936 an Irish Christian Front was created by Catholic groups sympathetic to Franco's Nationalist uprising in Spain. No major Catholic-inspired political movement did, however, emerge and instead it was through their influence over the two principal parties that Catholic ideas were most evident. Despite the Church's historic support for Cosgrave, once he was in office de Valera proved eager to demonstrate his Catholic credentials. He successfully fostered close links with the Church hierarchy and, when he introduced a new constitution in 1937, it made substantial gestures in the direction of Catholic ideas. Its preamble proclaimed the Catholic character of the Irish nation and, although it retained a system of democratic elections for the lower house of parliament, the composition of the upper house, the Senate, was based on the system of corporatist representation of professions and interest groups advocated by the papacy.

Catholic hostility to secular and democratic politics also made itself felt in Switzerland. While most Swiss Catholics had formerly tended to look on the federal and parliamentary constitution as the best means of defending their regional and confessional concerns, there was a marked shift within the Catholic population during the 1930s towards anti-democratic ideas. Influenced by neighbouring examples such as those of Italy and Austria, a number of Catholic intellectuals began to advocate a new social and political order based on distinctively Catholic principles. A predominantly Catholic Union Corporative Suisse (Swiss Corporatist Union) was founded in 1933 to campaign for corporatist ideas, and influential elements of the parliamentary Catholic Party, the KVP, including its youth wing, chose to affiliate themselves to the quasi-fascist National Front. In 1935 Catholic militants were a major force behind the referendum campaign to introduce a number of authoritarian and corporatist constitutional reforms and, although this was ultimately unsuccessful, it clearly demonstrated the rightward shift that had taken place in Catholic political loyalties during the 1930s.

The lure of a more 'authentic' Catholic social and political order also strongly influenced the Catholic movements of the newly independent states of central and eastern Europe. In Poland and Lithuania, the democratic constitutions established after the First World War had been overturned by coups in the mid-1920s which established the *de facto* dictatorships of Pilsudski in Poland and of Smetona in Lithuania. Both men were secular nationalists who, though not hostile to Catholicism, were reluctant to accord the Church and its affiliated organisations a privileged position in public life. Church–State conflicts over issues such as educational policy continued intermittently in both countries during the 1930s and encouraged many Catholics towards support for political reforms that would assert the pre-eminence of the Church and of the Catholic faith in national life. In Poland, the Church hierarchy had long supported the principal opposition force, the right-wing National Democrats, and, although Christian democrat ideas were popular among the Catholic workers of the industrial areas of Upper Silesia, the dominant trend in Catholic circles during the 1930s was emphatically towards authoritarian and corporatist ideas. Once again it was the young who came to the fore. Membership of Catholic Action groups in Poland exceeded one million by 1939 and it was intellectuals and university students, notably the influential Odrodzenie (Renaissance) movement, that popularised the ideas of a more militant Catholicism. This pattern was repeated in Lithuania where conflicts with the Smetona regime brought to the fore a new generation of leaders active in Catholic

Action movements and the powerful secondary school organisation, Ateitis (The Future). Strongly influenced by the Catholic intellectual trends of western Europe, these militants called for social and political reforms that would assert the Catholic character of the Lithuanian nation.

The interconnection of nationalism and religious identity was also the driving force behind Catholic politics in Slovakia and Croatia. Both were largely Catholic regions which, after the collapse of the Habsburg Empire in 1918, were subsumed in the predominantly non-Catholic states of Czechoslovakia and Yugoslavia respectively. Campaigns for greater cultural and political autonomy therefore went hand in hand with the assertion of the Catholic identity of the Slovak and Croatian peoples, and in both cases the Church and its affiliated organisations played a central role in encouraging the development of nationalist sentiments. In Slovakia throughout the inter-war years, the Slovak People's Party led by Hlinka, the Hlinkova slovenská l'udová strana (HSL'S), was the principal nationalist political movement, winning approximately 40 per cent of the votes of the Slovak population. The party had long been closely associated with the Catholic Church. Numerous priests were active in its ranks and, especially at a local level, it was the priesthood that often canvassed support for the HSL'S among the Catholic peasantry. Its propaganda also closely reflected its confessional origins. Denunciations of the Czech government's supposed neglect of the specific economic and cultural interests of Slovakia were combined with attacks on the anti-Catholic and so-called 'Hussite' character of the Czechoslovak state and on the disproportionate power exercised within Slovakia by a middle-class Lutheran minority. During the 1930s, the failure of its campaigns for a devolution of power to Slovakia exacerbated the long-standing divisions within the HSL'S. While some radicals began to look to Nazi Germany for support, much of the party nevertheless remained rooted in an intransigent and increasingly authoritarian Catholic nationalism reflected in its slogan 'One God, one People, one Party'.

A similar evolution was evident in the case of Croatia. Croatian grievances at the policies of the government in Belgrade and at the Serbian ascendancy which they appeared to symbolise had encouraged the development in the 1920s of parties, such as the Croatian Peasants' Party (Hrvatska Seljacka Stranka, HSS) led by the Radic brothers, which sought to defend Croatian interests within the Yugoslav state. But in the subsequent decade these were challenged by a more intransigent Croatian nationalism. The quasi-fascist Ustasa (Rising) movement, which was founded in 1929 by Ante Pavelić and was responsible in 1934 for the assassination of King Alexander of Yugoslavia, always remained, despite its notoriety, a relatively small organisation. Nevertheless, many of the authoritarian ideas of the Ustasa also found expression in Croatian Catholic social and spiritual associations. These expanded rapidly during the 1930s and received considerable encouragement from Archbishop Stepinac of Zagreb, a young prelate (aged only 34 in 1934) who had been strongly influenced by the pastoral ideas of Pius XI. Groups such as Krizari (Crusaders), a league of young Catholic militants which initially formed part of the Croatian Catholic Movement (the Hrvatski Katolicki Pokret, HKP) and – after its creation in 1934 – of Catholic Action, reflected the radicalism of a younger generation of Croatian Catholics for whom hostility to rule from Belgrade was inseparable from the establishment of an authoritarian Catholic social and political order in Croatia.

In Spain the fall of the dictatorship of Primo de Rivera in January 1930 and the subsequent founding of the Second Republic in April 1931 had plunged Catholics into a new and much less favourable political situation. The liberal rhetoric of the Republic's founders as well as outbursts of anti-clerical violence in some major urban centres provoked widespread apprehension among many Catholics, symbolised by the almost messianic fervour released by the repeated apparitions of the Virgin Mary in the small Basque village of Ezkioga during the summer of 1931. The Church hierarchy and almost all Catholic political leaders made no secret of their profound hostility to the new Republic. Nevertheless, its democratic national and local structures obliged Spanish Catholics to adopt the structures and trappings of modern mass politics. Acción Popular (Popular Action, AP), founded in 1931, was in effect the first national Catholic party of importance in Spain and it proved able to draw on the support not merely of established Catholic political groups but also of the powerful federation of Catholic agrarian syndicates, the CNCA, and of a wide range of Catholic social organisations, notably women's groups (who had been enfranchised by the Republic). This remarkable upsurge in Catholic political energies brought its reward in the elections of November 1933 when the new umbrella Catholic political organisation, the Confederación Española de Derechas Autónomas (the Spanish Confederation of Autonomous Right-Wing Groups, CEDA), which was the successor of the AP, emerged as the largest single party in the Republican parliament.

Not all Spanish Catholics were devoted to the abolition of the Republic and the democratic politics that it incarnated. Both among the former members of the short-lived PSP of the early 1920s and

Catalan and Basque Catholic organisations, most notably the Basque Nationalist Party (Partido Nacionalista Vasco, PNV), there were Catholics who were eager to explore the possibilities for Christian democratic politics which the Republic offered. For most Spanish Catholics there remained, however, a fundamental incompatibility between the Republic and the interests of Spanish Catholicism. The constitution of the Second Republic was emphatically, indeed aggressively, secular and its two principal supporters, the Radicals and the Socialists, regarded the malign influence of the Church as the principal obstacle to the modernisation of Spanish society. This polarisation between clericals and anti-clericals had been rooted in the tissues of Spanish urban and, more especially, provincial life since the mid-nineteenth century and it ensured that, despite the election victory of November 1933, the CEDA never embraced in anything more than name the pluralist politics of the Republic. The CEDA's ambition remained the reversal of the secular principles of the republican constitution and the establishment of a Catholic social and political order based around the Church, the monarchy and a network of socio-economic corporations.

For Catholic radicals throughout Europe, two regimes seemed to incarnate the values for which they were striving. The new constitutions established almost simultaneously by Salazar in Portugal and by Dollfuss in Austria in the early 1930s attracted enthusiastic and often extravagant praise from those Catholics who aspired to break with the social and political structures of the declining liberal world. This praise was not entirely unjustified: both regimes did indeed make much of their Catholic inspiration and combined authoritarian politics with promises of elaborate structures of professional corporations in which employers and workers would collaborate harmoniously in the pursuit of their common good. Nevertheless, the uncritical enthusiasm that events in Austria and Portugal aroused in Catholic circles elsewhere in Europe clearly owed less to the reality of these regimes than to the way in which Catholic radicals projected onto these distant experiments the reflection of their own aspirations. Neither Dollfuss nor Salazar was a simple Catholic idealist and, if the character of their regimes owed much to Catholic social and political ideas, they were also, above all, the product of particular national circumstances.

In the case of Portugal, the Estado Novo (New State) declared by Salazar in 1933 was the culmination of the gradual disintegration of the Republic established by the revolution of 1910. This republic – militantly anti-clerical in its ideology and urban and *petit bourgeois* in its basis of support – rapidly provoked a conservative backlash among the peasant smallholders of the north where levels of Catholic practice had long been markedly higher than in Lisbon and the largely dechristianised south of the country. A Catholic party, the Centro Católico Portuguesa (Portuguese Catholic Centre, CCP), was established in 1917 to defend Catholic and rural interests within the Republic but its moderate stance dissatisfied many Catholics for whom the primary objective remained the overthrow of the republican political structures. This was certainly true of the somewhat misleadingly titled Centro Academica da Democraçia Cristão (Academic Centre for Christian Democracy, CADC), founded in 1912 by intellectuals at the University of Coimbra, the historic centre of Portuguese Catholic intellectual life. With its slogan of 'Piety, study, action', the CADC became the focus for the energies of a new generation of politically ambitious and committed Catholics, including Salazar and Cerejeira, a priest and journalist who, at the remarkably young age of 41, was appointed in 1929 as the Archbishop of Lisbon. In May 1926, the parliamentary structures of the Republic were overthrown by a military coup and, after a period of chaotic military dictatorship, the militants of the CADC emerged as the nucleus of the new political order. Salazar, an economics professor at Coimbra, who had been minister of finance since 1928, was appointed as prime minister in 1932 and rapidly proceeded to liquidate the remains of the Republic.

Salazar's Estado Novo was a heterogeneous fusion of authoritarian models borrowed from foreign examples such as Fascist Italy and of the Catholic ideas of the CADC. A new authoritarian constitution and a single official party – the Uniao Nacional (National Union) – were created, and a National Labour Statute was proclaimed which claimed to replace liberal capitalism with a new economic structure of guilds and corporations. These were, however, merely the trappings of what always remained a highly personalised dictatorship. All power ultimately resided in the hands of Salazar and, although appeals to the Catholic heritage of Portugal and to the value of Catholic teachings were a continual point of reference in Salazar's public declarations, he was unwilling to accord the Church or Catholic associations any independence that would reduce his authority. The symbolism of Fatima, the site in central Portugal where the Virgin Mary appeared in 1917, was amply exploited by the regime as a symbol of Portuguese Catholic nationalism and the education system was remodelled as a vehicle of Catholic moral and social values. But Salazar was careful to keep his distance from the ecclesiastical hierarchy led by Cerejeira and the concordat signed by the regime and the papacy in 1940 accorded only relatively limited privileges to the Church.

In Austria, too, Catholicism was only one of the elements of the authoritarian regime which replaced the post-war Republic. Dollfuss, conscious of the precariousness of his political situation, certainly made energetic attempts to claim a Catholic legitimacy for his actions, declaring, for example, in a speech in September 1933 that 'The day of the capitalist–liberal economic order is past .... We demand a social, Christian, German Austria on a corporative basis and under strong authoritarian leadership.' It was this that the new constitution of 1934 was intended to provide. It appealed explicitly to Catholic values and consolidated the high regard in which Dollfuss was held by Catholics elsewhere in Europe. The papacy was particularly enthusiastic. Anxious to support Dollfuss as a bastion against Nazism in Austria, Pius XI declared unambivalently to Austrian pilgrims in Rome in 1933 that Dollfuss was 'a Christian, giant-hearted man ... who rules Austria so well, so resolutely and in such a Christian manner. His actions are witness to Catholic visions and convictions. The Austrian people, Our Beloved Austria, now has the government it deserves.'

Within Austria, however, Catholic attitudes were more circumspect. Certainly among both the laity and the ecclesiastical hierarchy there was considerable support for Dollfuss's action against the atheist Social Democrats. But the bishops were nervous about the ambitions of the regime to circumscribe the independence of Catholic Action and of Catholic youth movements, while many lay Catholics were left unimpressed by the efforts of Dollfuss to pose as the saviour of Catholic Austria. For all its Catholic rhetoric, the regime relied essentially on the institutional power of the bureaucracy, army and police, and Dollfuss's attempt in 1933 to launch a new official party, the Fatherland Front, aroused little popular enthusiasm. In July 1934, Dollfuss was killed in an abortive putsch by Austrian Nazis and his successor, Kurt von Schuschnigg, though equally eager to stress the Catholic inspiration for his actions, failed to invest the regime with a greater sense of purpose. Its bureaucratic authoritarianism was in many respects a nostalgic throwback to the methods of the Habsburg Empire of the nineteenth century, and when Hitler launched his unopposed invasion of Austria (the so-called *Anschluss*) in April 1938, the Schuschnigg government collapsed amidst general indifference.

A major reason for the uncritical enthusiasm with which many Catholics outside Portugal and Austria regarded the regimes of Salazar and Dollfuss was that they believed that they saw in them a Catholic alternative to fascism. The relationship between Catholic political movements of the 1930s and those of the secular extreme right was a complex one. Their shared hostility to liberal values and to structures of parliamentary democracy made them, in many respects, allies in a common cause and has led some historians such as Zeev Sternhell to regard the right-wing Catholic movements of the 1930s as little more than a constituent element of the wider phenomenon of fascism. But others – not least historians sympathetic to Catholicism – have taken issue with Sternhell's analysis and have been at pains to stress the points of divergence that remained between Catholic and fascist movements. As with many such historiographical debates, much of course depends upon where one begins. If one takes as one's starting point the assumption that there existed a clearly defined fascist phenomenon composed of a number of key characteristics, then it becomes relatively easy to demonstrate that many right-wing Catholic groups of the 1930s did indeed conform to this fascist model. If, however, one proceeds from an assumption that fascism was merely one of a variety of anti-democratic currents in inter-war Europe, it is more natural to portray the Catholic authoritarian movements of the era as co-existing alongside fascism without being subsumed by it.

More important perhaps than such problems of definition is the fact that Catholic militants of the 1930s *believed* that their ambitions and inspiration were different from those of the fascist extreme right. It was the cult of the state and, more especially, what they perceived to be the 'totalitarian' ambition of fascist movements to control all sectors of national life that many Catholics saw not merely as a threat to the autonomy of the Church but also as intrinsically inimical to Catholic teachings. Pius XI, in his pastoral letter *Non Abbiamo Bisogno* published in 1931 as well as in numerous other declarations, denounced the monstrosity of the notion that the individual existed only to serve the state, and his comments were echoed in the condemnations of fascist movements issued by many national ecclesiastical hierarchies. The establishment of the Nazi regime reinforced this antipathy to fascism, not merely among Catholics in those countries most directly threatened by an aggressive Germany but also elsewhere in Europe. The somewhat caricatured image of Nazism as a 'neo-pagan' religion and as a 'brown Bolshevism' – in other words on a par with the ultimate evil of Soviet communism – was widespread in the Catholic press of the era and considerable publicity was given to instances of persecution of the Catholic population in Germany by the Nazi authorities.

Their desire to define themselves against fascism encouraged Catholic movements to stress the uniqueness of Catholic political and social doctrine. The exclusivist and, in some extreme cases, almost messianic belief that Catholicism alone offered a solution to the manifold problems faced by the states of Europe, already evident in the

Catholic Action groups of the 1920s, became in the subsequent decade a central theme of Catholic rhetoric. Drawing on the substantial corpus of encyclicals issued on a wide range of subjects by the papacy over the previous fifty years, Catholic leaders of the 1930s insisted that they were the heirs to a distinctive Catholic political tradition which, by avoiding the twin perils of liberal individualism and Marxist or fascist totalitarianism, provided, so they claimed, a 'third way' for European societies. The problem resided, however, in providing these principles with a political definition. As we have seen, most (though certainly not all) Catholic movements in Europe during the 1930s gave a predominantly anti-parliamentary and corporatist interpretation to this Catholic tradition. But many points of tension remained. While young radicals, such as those of *Esprit* in France or the Rexists in Belgium, advocated a vaguely defined Catholic 'revolution', the political ambitions of many other Catholics remained rooted in a traditionalist conservatism and the defence of particular economic interests.

It was the issue of corporatism more than any other that expressed the ambivalence of Catholic political aspirations. No concept was more frequently invoked by Catholic movements during the 1930s, but none proved more evasive of concrete definition. It was Pius XI in his encyclical *Quadragesimo Anno* of May 1931 who made corporatism a central focus of Catholic political rhetoric. In what was without doubt his most important single encyclical, Pius used the fortieth anniversary of Leo XIII's encyclical *Rerum Novarum* to reaffirm the Church's fundamental opposition to the individualist principles of the capitalist economic system. The trend in the decades since the publication of *Rerum Novarum* towards monopolistic capitalism had, so Pius XI declared, reinforced the evil of liberal economic doctrines which divorced economic principles from personal morality. Adam Smith's comforting notion of the 'hidden hand' of the market, which ensured that the pursuit of self-interest worked for the good of all, held no appeal for the Pope. Instead, he advocated the introduction of a new economic structure which would replace the anarchic competition and class conflict of the classical liberal economy with a disciplined structure of corporations in which representatives of employers, of managers and of the workers within an individual factory or an industrial sector would resolve conflicts and learn to respect each other's interests.

Published in the depths of the economic Depression, *Quadragesimo Anno* had an immediate impact and its corporatist message was seized upon by Catholic groups throughout Europe as providing a Catholic solution to the economic crisis. A major element of its appeal lay, however, in its flexibility, not to say vagueness. While for some radicals, corporatism seemed to promise a decisive break with liberal political and economic values, many Catholic employers regarded it as little more than a reworking of traditional Catholic paternalism and a means of breaking the power of the trade unions. Catholic trade unionists regarded corporatist ideas with some suspicion and, although some Catholic technocrats presented corporatism as providing a rational structure for the modern economy, many of its advocates remained rooted in the neo-medieval nostalgia of the social Catholicism of the late nineteenth century. In these circumstances, it was scarcely surprising that where corporations were introduced, such as in Portugal and Fascist Italy, they proved to be largely ineffective. Far from providing the magic solution to class conflict and the economic crisis, they rapidly became unwieldy bureaucratic structures in which, not surprisingly, it was the interests of the employers that predominated.

While for many European Catholics the need to define their attitude towards fascism was primarily political or ideological, for Catholics in Italy and Germany (as well as in Austria from 1938) it was a much more immediate necessity. The Fascist and Nazi regimes not only dominated national life, they also invaded many areas of social and personal existence. It would be wrong to exaggerate the extent of their totalitarian control over society; both regimes were improvised and, in some respects, ineffectual structures, the pretensions of which to control all facets of society greatly exceeded their limited achievements. Nevertheless, for German and Italian Catholics in the 1930s Nazi and Fascist rule was an unavoidable reality and one that posed awkward choices between their obligations as a citizen and as a Catholic. Although many preferred to combine outward conformity with a certain internal withdrawal, these choices could not always be avoided. The propaganda of the regimes, their racial and anti-semitic policies and, during the Second World War, the requirement that millions of their citizens should fight for their cause required Catholics to confront – however obliquely – the issue of their attitude towards the established authorities. Debates about how far Italian and German Catholics 'collaborated' with or 'resisted' fascist rule fail to reflect, however, the complexity of Catholic responses. Black and white choices rarely presented themselves, and for most Catholics (as indeed for many of their fellow citizens of Italy and Germany) their actions during the Nazi and Fascist years were characterised by compromises, by moments of optimism and conviction and by much confusion.

In Italy, Catholic attitudes to the regime were inevitably much influenced by the oscillations in relations between the papacy and the Fascist state. Mussolini's opportunistic courting of papal support during his conquest of power had not pleased all elements among his supporters and throughout the 1920s there remained an influential anti-clerical wing of the Fascist Party associated with figures such as Farinacci and Balbo. Mussolini himself, however, while privately sharing the distrust of the Catholic Church felt by many Fascists, was eager to build a close (but not dependent) alliance with the papacy. Negotiations over the relationship between the Vatican and the Italian state, unresolved since national unification in the nineteenth century, began secretly in 1926 and reached a successful culmination with the dramatic announcement of the Lateran Treaties in 1929. While similar in form to the concordats signed by Pius XI with a considerable number of European states during his pontificate, these treaties also provided substantial financial compensation to the papacy for the loss of its territories in Italy and allowed the Church and its social organisations a significant degree of autonomy from state interference.

The Lateran Treaties were a considerable coup for Mussolini. They consolidated his regime within Italy and did much to improve his prestige abroad. Nevertheless, the price that he had paid for what amounted to a papal seal of approval was, in the eyes of many Fascists, too high. In particular, the freedom allowed to Catholic Action movements soon led to conflicts between the state and young Catholics. In May 1931 Mussolini ordered the dissolution of Catholic youth movements in violation of the Lateran Treaties, prompting the outspoken attack by Pius XI on the totalitarian ideology of the Fascist regime in the Italian-language encyclical *Non Abbiamo Bisogno*. The conflict was resolved by a further compromise agreement between the papacy and the Fascist regime in September 1931 which allowed Catholic Action groups to operate while seeking to ensure that their activities remained purely spiritual in nature. Nevertheless, an undercurrent of institutional tension remained in relations between the papacy and the Fascist state throughout the 1930s and reached a further crisis in 1938, prompted by Mussolini's introduction of antisemitic legislation inspired by Nazi examples and by the attempts of the Fascist state to reinforce its faltering authority by renewing its attacks on Catholic Action.

Rather like the papacy, many Italian Catholics combined a respect for certain of the achievements of the regime with a distrust of its statist and authoritarian methods. Especially among much of the Catholic middle class, the perception of Mussolini as the man who –

whatever his evident personal failings – had saved Italy from socialist rule and had restored the nation's international reputation proved to be a durable one. Active Catholic involvement in the regime was, however, limited. The so-called 'clerico-fascists' who had defected from the PPI to support Fascism had, by the mid-1920s, largely disappeared, and most Catholics withdrew from politics into the substantial network of Catholic social and cultural associations. After the conclusion of the Lateran Treaties, these came to form an influential alternative forum for Catholic activity and discussion. Catholic Action groups claimed a membership of one million by 1930 and were a reflection of what became during the 1930s a mood of Catholic revival in Italy. Though primarily spiritual in nature, this also had political and anti-Fascist connotations. Catholic associations and the Catholic press voiced coded but unambivalent criticisms of the regime, and organisations such as the Catholic student movement, the Federazione Universitari Cattolici Italiani (Federation of Italian Catholic University Students, FUCI), became a focus for the activities of the future leadership of the Christian Democrat Party which emerged in Italy after the overthrow of Mussolini in 1943.

Nevertheless, it would be wrong to exaggerate the degree of Catholic alienation from the Mussolini regime. There remained many points of convergence between Catholicism and Fascism. Mussolini's strong anti-communism, the neo-colonial invasion of Ethiopia in 1935 and the Italian military intervention in Spain in 1936 to support Franco's uprising were all factors on which the Fascist state and most Catholics shared a similar attitude. Only among the Catholic working class of the northern industrial regions had a profound distrust of Mussolini's oppression of workers' rights produced, prior to the war years, what was a clear Catholic rejection of Fascism.

In Germany, relations between Catholicism and the Nazi state continued to be dominated by the atmosphere of mutual distrust that had been evident during the years preceding the Nazi acquisition of power. Despite the quiescence of the Catholic ecclesiastical and political leadership in Hitler's dismantling of the Weimar political structures and the concordat signed between Nazi Germany and the papacy in 1933, both sides regarded each other with guarded suspicion. The hierarchy of the Church, represented by the Fulda Bishops Conference, acted cautiously. It reiterated its loyalty to the new order (including notoriously sending fulsome birthday greetings to Hitler) while at the same time seeking to use the provisions of the concordat to maintain the Church's cultural and social organisations. Conversely, the Nazi rulers initially sought to avoid any direct conflict with the

Church but, from 1935 onwards, felt sufficiently confident of their position to begin to erode Catholic autonomy. A series of sexual and financial scandals allegedly involving members of the clergy were energetically exploited by the Nazi-controlled press, and Catholic youth movements were harried by the police into abandoning their activities.

The deep concern felt by Pius XI at the persecution of the Catholic Church in Germany led him to compose a forthright attack on Nazi methods and ideology entitled *Mit brennender Sorge* (With Burning Concern) which was dramatically read to the faithful from pulpits throughout Germany on Palm Sunday, 14 March 1937. Although it had few practical consequences, the papal statement reinforced the Nazi perception of the Catholic Church and, indeed, of the Catholic population in general as a potential threat to their authority. Nazi police reports from Catholic regions of Germany such as the Rhineland and Bavaria frequently dwelt on the suspect attitudes of Catholic priests and laity, and in the *Kristallnacht* (Crystal Night) violence of November 1938 when Nazi gangs attacked many Jewish buildings, the palaces of the bishops of Munich and Vienna were also ransacked.

Nevertheless, it would be misleading to portray – as some Catholic historians have tended to do – the relationship between the regime and the Catholic Church and laity as one of increasingly bitter conflict. As war approached, the Nazis muted their attacks on the Catholic Church in order to reinforce national solidarity, and when further points of conflict subsequently arose, notably over the euthanasia and sterilisation programmes directed against the mentally ill and the ham-fisted attempts of the Nazi authorities to remove crucifixes from school classrooms, Hitler proved willing to make gestures to appease the Catholic Church. Similarly, although the Catholic bishops voiced criticisms of the 'pagan' racial policies of the Nazis, these were accompanied by professions of loyalty to the regime and, from September 1939, by active support for the German war effort. Thus, there remained throughout the era of the Third Reich a cautious *modus vivendi* between the Church and the Nazi state which, on the Catholic side, was rooted in the distinctive historical experience of Catholics as a minority within the German population. Just as they had done during Bismarck's attacks on the Catholic Church in the 1870s, the Catholic authorities responded to persecution by seeking to protect the Church and faithful while repeatedly proclaiming their higher loyalty to the German Reich.

The Catholic laity similarly sought to combine muted criticism with nervous expressions of their patriotic commitment. Although student groups and some Catholic workers' organisations did not disguise their antipathy to the Nazi regime and engaged in open displays of defiance, these were minority attitudes. Most German Catholics reacted to Nazi actions by simply keeping their heads down. Catholic spiritual associations flourished during the Third Reich and provided a discreet and uncontroversial means of maintaining Catholic loyalties. Retreats and pilgrimages, such as those to the site of the apparition of the Virgin Mary at Marpingen in the Saarland, enabled Catholics to affirm their religious identity while at the same time reflecting a tacit disapproval of Nazi secular violence. This internal and, in many respects, only semi-conscious distancing from Nazism was also evident in the emphatic localism of much Catholic (and indeed Protestant) activity during the years of the Third Reich. German Catholics withdrew from national affairs into the regional life of the predominantly Catholic areas of southern and western Germany. Such localism did not exclude a sense of 'Germanness' but it provided an alternative to the aggressive nationalism of the Nazi regime. Rooted in these overlapping and largely complementary Catholic and regional identities, the Catholic experience of Nazism was more passive than active. Their stance was less one of clear-cut opposition than of surviving and of getting by.

The political stance adopted by Catholics in Spain during the 1930s was in almost every respect the opposite of that in Germany. While German Catholics always regarded Nazism as an essentially alien force, in Spain a large majority of Catholics rallied enthusiastically to Franco's Nationalist military uprising against the Second Republic in July 1936. Apart from demonstrating the vacuity of simplistic definitions of fascism which seek to reduce all movements of the extreme right to a few common denominators, the contrast in Catholic attitudes towards Hitler and Franco also reflected the very different mentalities of Catholics in the two countries. In Germany, Catholics were a minority seeking to defend their rights; in Spain, by contrast, the goal of Catholics was to rescue their country from the control of revolutionary and atheist forces. Despite the electoral victory of the Catholic party (the CEDA) in November 1933, most Catholics never saw their participation in the politics of the Second Republic as anything more than a lesser evil. Their stance remained what the leader of the CEDA, Gil Robles, proclaimed to be an 'unyielding repugnance' for the principles of the Republic and a commitment to the re-establishment of the true Catholic Spain.

Any lingering hope that political Catholicism might be reconciled with the democratic and pluralist principles of the Republic disappeared when, in the elections of February 1936, the forces of the right

were decisively defeated by a left-wing Popular Front. Anti-clerical
Radicals came into government, while in the streets of Barcelona and
Madrid the Communists and Anarchists constituted an increasingly
powerful presence. Among Catholics, the victory of the left fulfilled
their worst nightmares. The defence of bourgeois class interests against
the spectre of social revolution and of rural property against the
collectivisation of land by the 'red' government fused with fears of the
persecution of the Church by what was perceived to be a regime of
Marxists, freemasons and Jews. In response, many younger Catholics
rallied to the extreme-right militia, the Falange, while the Catholic
authorities called ever more explicitly for a saviour who would rescue
Spain from its enemies.

When the Spanish military launched their rising against the
Republic in July 1936, Catholic support for their cause was, thus, as
Mary Vincent has remarked, a 'foregone conclusion'. However, the
failure of the rebels to capture the principal cities transformed the
coup into a bloody Civil War which lasted until the spring of 1939.
Within the Republican-controlled territories, the news of the uprising
provoked an outpouring of violence against those believed to support
the military rebels. Thirteen bishops, more than 4,000 parish priests
and 2,648 members of religious orders (including 283 nuns) were
murdered in the summer of 1936. This anti-clerical violence, without
parallel in the history of twentieth-century Europe, only served to
render even more emphatic the Catholic identification with Franco.
There remained certain rare exceptions. In the Basque country, the
Catholic party, the PNV, rallied to the Republican cause against the
centralising Spanish nationalism of Franco while certain Catholic
intellectuals remained loyal to the democratic principles of the
Republic, especially in the face of the Nationalist rebels' increasing
reliance on the military assistance of Fascist Italy and Nazi Germany.
Overwhelmingly, however, Spanish Catholics supported the
Nationalist cause, by fighting in its armies or organising resistance in
Republican-held territories to the legitimate government. A collective
letter, signed by most of the Spanish bishops, proclaimed that God
was on the Nationalist side and Franco returned the compliment by
presenting his rebellion as a crusade to restore the Church and
Catholic values in Spain.

The energy and commitment with which most Spanish Catholics
supported the Nationalist cause were a reaction to the secular policies
of the Republic and to fear of social revolution. It was, however, also
deeply rooted in the anti-modern character of Spanish Catholicism.
More so than anywhere else in Europe, Catholics in Spain remained

loyal to a traditional vision of an integral Catholic order, more charac-
teristic of the nineteenth century than of the twentieth. Fidelity to the
Church went hand in hand with a nostalgic vision of a rural Spanish
people united in loyalty to their monarch, which bore little resem-
blance to the reality of a more urban, industrial and diverse society.
There were several reasons for what might be termed this Spanish
peculiarity. To some extent, its origins can be traced back to the traumatic impact of Napoleon's invasion of Spain in 1808 and the abrupt
imposition of a modern liberalism identified with the foreign enemy.
Throughout the nineteenth century, attitudes to liberal reforms
provided the principal fault line of Spanish political debate, and
Catholicism became a central structural and ideological component of
opposition to the social and political modernisation of Spain. In
opting for Franco in 1936, Spanish Catholics were therefore acting in
accordance with this historical tradition. Their choice was, however,
also determined by the social structure of Catholicism in Spain. In the
major cities, the reactionary stance of the Church on many social
issues and its slowness to respond to the growth of new industrial
suburbs had accelerated the dechristianisation of the working class
while reinforcing middle-class self-identification in the values of
Catholicism. In rural Spain, the patterns of the Catholic faith were
similarly moulded by social and economic realities. In southern areas
such as Andalusia, where much of the population worked as hired
labourers on the large estates, religious practice was low, while in
northern regions such as old Castille and Navarre, where small land-
holdings were the norm, loyalty to Catholicism was inseparable from
hostility to liberal governments in Madrid unsympathetic to the
concerns of peasant farmers.

The reaction of Catholics outside Spain to the Nationalist military
uprising was initially largely similar to that of Spanish Catholics.
Knowledge of the background to events in Spain was limited and the
sensational news coverage of the attacks on the Spanish clergy encouraged many European Catholics to regard Franco as a Catholic leader
akin to Salazar and Dollfuss. In contrast, Catholics opposed the
Republic because of its violently anti-clerical reputation, but also more
especially because of what they perceived to be its quasi-communist
character. It is almost impossible to exaggerate the extent to which a
visceral anti-communism formed part of the mentality of Catholics in
inter-war Europe. Events in Russia in 1917 as well as the revolutionary
upheavals in central Europe after the First World War had conjured up
the spectre of Soviet Bolshevism as the ultimate enemy, devoted to the
extirpation of all forms of religious belief and the installation of a

bleak totalitarian order. Pius XI, whose experiences as papal nuncio in Poland during the Soviet–Polish War of 1919–20 had done much to reinforce his own antipathy to communism, presented the communist danger in almost apocalyptic terms, declaring in the encyclical *Divini Redemptoris*, published in the midst of the Spanish Civil War in March 1937, that communism was an 'intrinsically perverse' doctrine with which Catholics could have no contact. At a time when many others in Europe were still inclined to see positive features of the Soviet experiment, the Catholic condemnation of atheist Bolshevism was categorical, and crude anti-communist stereotypes predominated in the Catholic press of the 1930s.

Catholic support outside Spain for the Nationalists focused therefore on Franco's role as the defender of Spain and of the Catholic faith against communist revolution. Although the Vatican cautiously avoided going too far in its diplomatic recognition of the rebels, many other Catholics were much less inhibited. Among Catholic intellectuals, notably in France, there were some who stood out against the trend, drawing attention to Nationalist atrocities and rallying support for the Basque Catholics opposed to Franco. But they were lone voices. Much more common were Catholic eulogies of Franco as a new El Cid, a chivalrous knight riding to rescue Spain from the Marxist barbarism of the Republic. This created some strange political alliances. Catholic organisations in the Netherlands, for example, found themselves echoing Dutch extreme-right groups in their support for the Nationalists, while in Britain Cardinal Hinsley of Westminster, though certainly no friend of fascism, kept a signed photograph of Franco displayed on his desk even during the Second World War.

In many respects, this naively positive image of Franco remained current up to, and indeed beyond, the end of the Civil War in 1939. Support for the Nationalist cause did, however, gradually become more muted among Catholics outside Spain as they became aware of their reliance on Italian and German military aid. Nationalist atrocities, including most notoriously the bombing of the town of Guernica in April 1937, tarnished Franco's image and, although many non-Spanish Catholics were still convinced that the Nationalists were preferable to the atheist Republicans, they were unwilling to appear to support the aggressive policies of the fascist powers. Events in Spain, it became increasingly clear, could not be separated from the diplomatic conflict in Europe, and what had seemed initially to be a just war of Catholic defence came to be part of the wider struggle between fascism and its democratic and left-wing opponents.

The impossibility of divorcing events within one country from the menacing international climate also made itself felt elsewhere in Europe during the late 1930s. This was especially so in France, where politics followed a superficially similar (though much less bloody) course to that in Spain. The victory of a Popular Front coalition of centre-left Radicals, Socialists and Communists in the elections of May 1936 and the subsequent establishment of a Radical–Socialist government supported by the Communists and headed by the veteran Socialist leader Léon Blum could scarcely fail to alarm French Catholics. Divided on many issues of social and economic policy, the coalition relied for its coherence on a shared loyalty to the heritage of the Revolution of 1789 and the Republicanism of the nineteenth century. Not surprisingly, therefore, the Popular Front government was perceived by many Catholics as heralding a return to the bitter Church–State conflicts of the 1890s and 1900s. In fact, such fears proved to be largely unjustified. Unlike its equivalent in Spain, the Popular Front in France did little to enflame Catholic sensibilities and, in a spectacular gesture, the Communist leader Maurice Thorez issued an appeal to French Catholics in April 1936 to work with the Communist Party to achieve a more just society.

La main tendue (the outstretched hand) offered by Thorez was, however, not reciprocated. With the exception of a few highly unrepresentative groups such as the self-styled Catholic revolutionaries of *Terre Nouvelle* (New Land), French Catholic opinion remained united in its opposition to the Popular Front. There were nuances in their attitudes. The Christian democrats of the Parti Démocrate Populaire (PDP), although they voted against the Blum government, attempted to adopt a stance of constructive criticism towards its social reforms, while those Catholic intellectuals associated with periodicals such as *Esprit*, *L'Aube* and *Sept* combined opposition to the Popular Front with calls for Catholics to reject their historic antipathy to the Third Republic. Mainstream Catholic opinion, as represented by the large-circulation and conservative titles such as *La France catholique* (Catholic France), was, however, unambivalent in its rejection of the Popular Front. A long-standing distrust of the intrigues of freemasonic and anti-clerical politicians fused in Catholic minds with the more novel theme of anti-communism. The impact of the Spanish Civil War was felt more strongly in neighbouring France than anywhere else in Europe and many Catholics saw alarming parallels between communist influence within Republican Spain and the support of the French Communist Party for the Blum government and its prominent role within the trade union movement. For many

Catholics, the noisy street politics and the relatively modest social reforms of 1936 did seem to be the first steps on a slippery slope to revolution and, although the Popular Front had effectively come to an end by the summer of 1937, the fears that it conjured up go far towards explaining the initial enthusiasm with which many Catholics subsequently greeted Maréchal Pétain's seizure of power in 1940.

Though united in opposition to the Popular Front, French Catholics were, however, unable to agree on many other issues. Compared with the other major Catholic nations of Europe, the major anomaly of France remained the absence of a Catholic party of importance. The PDP was a stagnant force limited to its Christian democratic clientele, while most French Catholics, such as the peasant farmers of the west, continued to vote for secular parties of the right, notably the Fédération Républicaine (Republican Federation) which combined defence of the Church with the protection of rural interests. Indeed, in many respects, the possibility of a major Catholic party emerging in France receded substantially during the 1930s. The international and domestic crises of the decade accentuated the fissures within French Catholicism between Christian democrats and conservatives and between the intellectual elite and the predominantly rural and bourgeois laity. By the end of the decade, Catholic politics was effectively polarised between a minority of Christian democrats and a majority who remained rooted in the conservative and anti-republican prejudices of the turn of the century. Communication between the two was almost impossible. Especially after the outbreak of the Spanish Civil War, Christian democrats associated with the periodical *L'Aube*, edited by Francisque Gay, or with the closely related movement, the Nouvelles Equipes Françaises (New Leaders of France), established in 1938, were regarded by many other Catholics as traitors to their faith because of their refusal to condemn the Spanish Republicans. Conversely, attitudes hardened among the conservative majority during the pre-war years. There was a resurgence in support for the authoritarian ideas represented by newspapers such as *Action Française* and Catholic militants, such as the young François Mitterrand, provided much of the personnel of the various parties and leagues active on the extreme right of the French political spectrum.

The bitter divisions among French Catholics were symptomatic of the difficulties experienced by Catholic movements throughout Europe during the late 1930s. The pressure of international events and, more especially, the gradual realisation of the possibility of a new general war in Europe made it difficult for Catholic political movements to maintain their momentum. From the summer of 1936 until the even-tual outbreak of war between Nazi Germany and the Western Allies three years later, domestic politics in almost all European states became dominated by the succession of diplomatic crises and the impending military conflict that they appeared to herald. National loyalties took precedence over partisan conflicts and there was a decline in Catholic militancy as attention turned from projects of social and political reform to more pressing issues of military defence. In common with almost all Europeans, Catholics looked on the prospect of war with quiet despair. Fear of war and, more especially, of the impact of new technologies of warfare, such as the aerial bombing of civilian populations, gave a new urgency to prayers for peace and led the papacy to call on the major powers to settle their differences by peaceful means. For the Church leaders, as well as for many ordinary Catholics, the drift towards war seemed to be expressive of the errors of a modern atheist and materialist society which had rejected the teachings of the Christian faith. Unlike in 1914, few Catholics were eager to invoke theological notions of a just war and, though integral pacifism remained the choice of only a tiny minority, both the Church and many Catholic movements became associated to an unprecedented degree with a principled opposition to war.

Moral scruples were reinforced by more political considerations. The polarisation of Europe into two mutually antagonistic fascist and democratic blocs posed in a particularly stark form the fundamental choice that many Catholic movements of the 1930s had sought to avoid. Hostile to both the centralised dictatorships of Nazi Germany and Fascist Italy and the secular liberalism of the Western powers, the neutrality of many Catholics was as much a political as a moral choice. They identified fully with neither camp and hoped instead for some form of mediated settlement which would avert a military conflict. The scope for any form of so-called 'third way', be it political or diplomatic, was, however, steadily eroded by the logic of the diplomatic crisis. The Dollfuss–Schuschnigg regime in Austria was overthrown by the German invasion of April 1938 and Salazar's Portugal withdrew into a prudent isolationism, while elsewhere in Europe the radical Catholic movements that had emerged during the 1930s either evaporated or moved significantly away from their original inspiration. The Slovak People's Party emerged as the ruler of an independent Slovak state under German patronage in March 1939 and in Belgium Léon Degrelle's Rexist movement destroyed much of its credibility by seeking to convert itself from a movement of Catholic populism into an extreme-right party, crudely modelled on Nazi and Italian examples.

By the eve of war, the expansion of Catholic politics that had taken place in Europe during the preceding twenty years had therefore been substantially, if only temporarily, reversed. Apart from in the Iberian peninsula and the Low Countries, Catholic movements were either in opposition or had been forcibly dissolved by authoritarian regimes. The optimism and political commitment so evident among many Catholics earlier in the decade had disappeared and their energies transferred to new priorities. In much of Europe during the pre-war years there was an upsurge in devotional and spiritual movements which, by consciously turning their back on an alien and unsympathetic world, sought to foster among their members a more intense religious life. These groups marked a change of mentality within Catholicism: the militant triumphalist rhetoric of the Catholic Action movements of the 1920s and early 1930s had gone out of fashion and, especially among younger Catholics, there was an evolution towards a more personal and individual definition of their Catholic faith.

This change was, in many respects, no more than a reaction to adverse circumstances. The years of the Second World War would provide ample evidence that the militancy of the inter-war years remained a powerful force within Catholic ranks. Nevertheless, the evolution that began to manifest itself during the late 1930s was also a precursor of the Christian democracy of the post-1945 era. The purposes of Catholic politics were beginning to change almost imperceptibly. Catholic political action during the 1920s and 1930s had focused on the twin goals of the defence of the Church and the achievement of a new social and political order based on Catholic principles. But the immediate pre-war years witnessed the tentative emergence of a new perception of Catholics, not as defenders of the Church or advocates of a distinctive social and political programme, but as Christian citizens acting within society without seeking to impose their values on it. This new mentality would come to the fore after the Second World War; but it had already begun to take shape in the difficult circumstances of the pre-war years.

BIBLIOGRAPHICAL NOTES

The tensions imposed by the Depression on Catholic politics are illustrated with reference to Belgium by Gerard (1986), Stengers (1965) and Conway (1996b). Edmondson (1976), Carsten (1977) and Weinzierl (1987) chart the decline of the Christian Socials and the rise of the Heimwehr in Austria. In Germany, the rightward shift of the Centre Party is well illustrated by Patch (1985) and Moeller (1986). Morsey

(1977) analyses the actions of the party in the months prior to Hitler's appointment as chancellor, while Schönhoven (1977) demonstrates the BVP's support for an alliance with the NSDAP. Mühlberger (1987) assesses membership of the NSDAP, and Catholic student attitudes to Nazism are considered by Grüttner (1995). Falter (1991) and Childers (1983) provide evidence of general Catholic under-representation among the electorate of the NSDAP; Heilbronner (1992), Osmond (1993) and Zofka (1986) illustrate some of the many exceptions to this rule. Von Hehl (1992), Lönne (1996) and Stehlin (1983) examine the actions of the Centre Party and the Church hierarchy in the crucial months following the Nazi acquisition of power.

The lively Catholic intellectual culture in France is described in Coutrot (1961), Winock (1975) and Hellman (1981). Sternhell (1986) stresses Catholic infatuation with ideas of the extreme right in France. Similar developments in Belgium are considered in Etienne (1968), Vos (1982) and Conway (1990) and in the Netherlands in Beaufays (1973) and Luykx (1978). Dunphy (1995), Lee (1989) and Keogh and O'Driscoll (1996) discuss Irish Catholic politics; the Blueshirt movement is analysed by Cronin (1994). Swiss Catholic attitudes are examined in Altermatt (1979), Evans (1984) and Ruffieux (1969). Events in Poland are the subject of Polonsky (1972), Pease (1991) and Przeciszewski (1988) and those in Lithuania of Vardys (1965 and 1978) and Von Rauch (1974). The interconnection of Catholicism and nationalism in Slovakia and Croatia is demonstrated with reference to the former by Mamatey (1973), Felak (1994) and Hoensch (1987) and to the latter by Crampton (1994), Alexander (1987) and Jelinek (1980). Spanish Catholic hostility to the founding of the Second Republic is amply illustrated by Lannon (1987), Christian (1996) and Vincent (1989). Robinson (1970) and Vincent (1996a) provide contrasting descriptions of the CEDA while Preston (1994) situates it in the context of Spanish political life. Vincent (1996b) is an excellent study of local Catholic attitudes.

The origins and nature of the Salazar regime in Portugal are considered in Wheeler (1978), Gallagher (1983 and 1996) and Pinto (1995). Studies of the Dollfuss regime in Austria include those of Carsten (1977), Rath (1971) and Miller (1988). Rhodes (1973) illustrates papal enthusiasm while Gellott (1988) examines the more circumspect stance of the Austrian Church hierarchy. Bukey (1986) is an illuminating local study. The complex relationship between Catholicism and fascism has given rise to considerable debate. Sternhell (1986) presents the prosecution case; Chélini (1983) and Comte (1985) that for the defence. Payne (1980) and Griffin (1991) seek to relate Catholicism to the elusive concept of fascism while Hobsbawm (1994), Wolff and Hoensch (1987) and Conway (1990) argue for the existence of a distinct Catholic anti-democratic current in Europe during the 1930s. Papal condemnations of fascist totalitarianism are illustrated by Agostino (1991) and Holmes (1981). Michel (1987), Gergely (1987) and Christophe (1989) give examples of the negative image of Nazism in Catholic circles in the 1930s.

The encyclical *Quadragesimo Anno* is discussed by Schuck (1991). Evidence of the enthusiastic response it provoked is provided by Régnier (1991), Gergely (1980) and Ruffieux (1969). The infatuation with corporatism in the 1930s is explored with reference to Belgium by Luyten (1990); Gallagher (1983) demonstrates its unimpressive reality in Portugal.

General accounts of Italian Fascism include those of Morgan (1995) and De Grand (1989). Pollard (1985) and O'Brien (1982) chart the ebbs and flows in relations between Mussolini and the papacy. The variety of Catholic lay attitudes to the Fascist regime is illustrated by Pollard (1990 and 1996), De Grazia (1981) and Pecorari (1979). German Catholicism during the years of the Third Reich is surveyed by Von Hehl (1992), Lönne (1996) and, for the war years, by Kitchen (1995). Helmreich (1979) provides a comprehensive account of relations between the Church hierarchy and the regime; Noakes (1978) analyses the conflicts provoked by Nazi attempts to remove crucifixes from schools. The origins and content of *Mit brennender Sorge* are explained in Holmes (1981) and Chadwick (1986). Grüttner (1995) and Patch (1985) explore student and worker attitudes respectively, while examples of local Catholic responses to Nazism are examined by Kershaw (1983) (Bavaria), Gellately (1990) (Franconia) and Blackbourn (1993) (the Saarland). Luza (1977) considers Austria after the *Anschluss*.

Vincent (1996a) gives a succinct account of Spanish Catholicism during the years of the Second Republic and Civil War. The essays by Ben-Ami (1984), Lannon (1984) and Fusi (1984) in the collection edited by Preston (1984) as well as that by Vincent (1989) illustrate aspects of Catholic reactions to the Republic. Preston (1994) provides a thorough political narrative of the years 1931–6. The Falange is studied by Ellwood (1987). Montero Moreno (1961) gives statistics of the victims of anti-clerical violence in 1936; its social context is illuminated by Seidman (1991) and Pasos (1987). Preston (1993) is an imposing biography of Franco. The historical and social origins of the conservatism of Spanish Catholicism can be explored through the works of Carr (1982), Lannon (1987), Callahan (1989) and the study of Carlism by Blinkhorn (1975). Papal diplomacy during the Civil War is the subject of Kent (1986) while Chélini (1983) and Rhodes (1973) demonstrate the profound anti-communism that suffused Catholicism. Rémond (1960), Tranvouez (1983b), Luykx (1996) and Buchanan (1997) analyse lay Catholic reactions outside Spain to the Civil War.

The history of the French Popular Front of the mid-1930s is studied by Jackson (1988); Catholic reactions to it are surveyed by Rémond (1960) and McMillan (1996a). The Communist *main tendue* and the small minority who grasped it are analysed by Murphy (1989). Delbreil (1990) describes the stance of the PDP, and Winock (1975) and Coutrot (1961) provide case studies of Catholic intellectual periodicals of the 1930s. The Fédération Républicaine is studied by Irvine (1979), while support for the extreme right on the part of Catholics in general and François Mitterrand in particular is considered by Soucy (1995) and Péan (1994) respectively. Catholic attitudes during the phoney war of 1939–40 are the subject of Christophe (1989).

Papal pleas for peace in the pre-war years are described in the fine study by Chadwick (1986). Felak (1994) analyses the Slovak path to independence while Etienne (1968) describes the decline of the Rexist movement in Belgium. The trend away from Catholic political engagement during the late 1930s is illustrated by the examples studied by Sauvage (1987), Trimouille (1991) and Dumons (1994).

4 Catholicism during the Second World War
A changed continuity

The years of the Second World War remain a strangely neglected period of the political history of twentieth-century Europe. Amidst the attention lavished by historians on the battles, diplomacy and social history of the war years, there has been a tendency to overlook the politics of the period or, at best, to regard it as of only secondary importance. But politics did not stop when the war began in September 1939 in order to begin again when the guns finally fell silent in May 1945. Although the war was an inescapable presence in the lives of Europeans during these years, it also remained for much of the period strangely distant. In this global conflict, the war took place in the skies over their heads, in the icy waters of the North Atlantic or, for a number of years, on the fringes of Europe on the battlefields of North Africa or Russia. Europeans were intimately engaged both physically and emotionally in all of these conflicts; the sound of battle was, however, largely absent from their lives. From 1943 onwards the development of guerrilla warfare by Resistance movements and the successive Allied invasions of southern, eastern and western Europe remorselessly brought the war, with its manifold choices and dangers, to the heart of Europe. But, for much of the period, a tenuous normality reigned in the lives of many Europeans. The consequences of the war were all around them, but so too were the familiar structures of daily life. Political life also continued. If there were no elections and few parliaments, politics nevertheless continued by other means. Censored and clandestine newspapers sustained public debate and local government acquired a heightened importance in people's lives, while major political events, such as the creation of the Vichy regime in France in 1940 or the overthrow of Mussolini in Italy in 1943, animated private and public conversations.

This continuation of old patterns of life amid new challenges, which characterised the war years in Europe, prevailed also in the Catholic politics of the period. There was no such thing as a common Catholic experience of the war. Catholics fought in large numbers on both sides: in the Italian and German armies as well as in numerous smaller volunteer units for the Axis cause; in the armies of France, the Low Countries and Poland, among many others, for the Allies. At the same time, four major Catholic countries of Europe – Spain, Portugal, Switzerland and the Irish Republic – retained an occasionally somewhat tenuous neutrality throughout the conflict. The impact of the war was also profoundly unequal. In Poland, Catholics found themselves plunged into the unremitting nightmare of Nazi attempts to extirpate all aspects of Polish national life, while in Croatia and Slovakia the accidents of war enabled the attainment of national independence and a mood of Catholic triumphalism. In the neutral states as well as in Germany and Italy, Catholic life proceeded for the majority of the period relatively untouched by the consequences of war, while in those areas of Europe occupied by the Axis powers the Catholic Church and laity were obliged to make new and often difficult political choices. Some opted for resistance; a few opted for collaboration; most sought merely to survive.

The consequences of the war for Catholic politics were similarly diverse. The sufferings of the war years and the enforced opportunities that they provided for contact between Catholics and their fellow citizens did much to erode – at least temporarily – the 'ghetto mentality' which had for so long characterised Catholic political life. The consequence was a new openness to non-Catholic ideas which found expression in the non-confessional political initiatives of the post-war years. At the same time, however, the war reinforced old fears. The military advance of the Red Army into the Catholic heart of Europe and the unprecedented levels of support for communist parties in many areas of southern and western Europe gave a new strength to Catholic anti-communism. Communism might be a lesser evil than Nazism but for many Catholics it remained a close-run thing. Nervousness of a communist ascendancy helped to anchor the loyalties of many Catholics firmly on the right of the political spectrum and, together with fears that the predominantly left-wing governments of the post-war era would return to the anti-clerical policies of the past, ensured that Catholic politics emerged from the war dominated as much by old anxieties as by new opportunities.

Throughout the war, the papacy retained a careful neutrality. Pius XI died in February 1939 and his successor, Pius XII, elected the following month, was a cautious Vatican diplomat wedded to a traditional and hierarchical vision of the Catholic Church. Ascetic, austere and highly conscious of the majesty of his office, the new Pope eschewed the grand gestures of his predecessor. He preferred private diplomacy to public statements and, although his first encyclical *Summi Pontificatus*, published in October 1939, criticised in guarded terms the totalitarian methods of Nazism, he never clearly condemned German wartime aggressions. This silence, as well as the failure of the papacy to act decisively on the information it received of Nazi atrocities against Jewish populations in Europe, continues to arouse considerable controversy. Pius XII had served as the papal nuncio in Munich and subsequently Berlin from 1917 to 1929 and he retained from that era a deep affection for German culture. His wartime neutrality was thus of the heart as well as of the head. Although he refused to give his blessing to the German 'crusade' against the Soviet Union in 1941, he never-theless did not hesitate to criticise certain Allied actions, such as the bombing of Rome in the summer of 1943. Above all, Pius XII called for peace. Bringing an end to the war was for him a priority which took precedence over all others, including the defeat of Nazism. In his public statements, he repeatedly called on the belligerents to lay down their weapons and in private he encour-aged attempts to favour a compromise peace, acting for example during the 'phoney war' of 1939–40 as an intermediary in the unsuccessful secret discussions between the Western powers and German generals opposed to Hitler.

The German attack on Poland in September 1939 marked the beginning of the Second World War but, after a winter of uneasy silence, it was the German invasion of western Europe in May 1940 that decisively swept away any lingering hopes of peace. The rapid defeat by the German armies of the Netherlands, of Belgium and, above all, of France in June appeared to transform the balance of power in Europe. With British troops expelled from the European continent, the United States still neutral and the Soviet Union tied to Nazi Germany by the non-aggression pact of 1939, there appeared to be little realistic chance that the German hegemony in western Europe would be reversed. The populations of the Low Countries and France therefore sought, as best they could, to come to terms with their new situation. In France, Maréchal Pétain swept away the discredited struc-tures of the Third Republic and established a new French state committed to collaboration with Germany, while in Belgium and the Netherlands the political and administrative elites sought to negotiate the retention of national sovereignty within a German-dominated New Order Europe.

The Catholic Church and laity formed an important element of the new political structure that emerged in western Europe in the summer of 1940. As one of the few institutions to have survived the German invasion relatively intact, the Church acquired a greater prominence in public life and Catholic individuals and social organisations were to the fore in the political initiatives of the time. In the Netherlands, Dutch Catholics were active in the Nederlandse Unie (Dutch Union), a mass movement established in the summer of 1940 which, although it maintained its distance from the supporters of collaboration, was strongly influenced by corporatist and anti-democratic ideas. Similarly, in Belgium, the Church hierarchy firmly supported the stance of those such as King Léopold III (who had chosen to remain in the country in May 1940, rather than fleeing into exile) who believed that the national defeat had vindicated the need for certain New Order reforms. Catholics were prominent in the new social and economic organisations set up in Belgium during the Occupation and many Catholic trade unionists joined the new official trade union established with German support.

It was, however, indisputably in France that the impact of Catholicism on politics was most emphatic. The dissolution of the Third Republic and its replacement in July 1940 by a new authoritarian regime based at Vichy headed by the octogenarian military hero Maréchal Pétain was heralded by many French Catholics almost as a manifestation of divine providence. After the chaos of the German invasion and the humiliating armistice concluded by the French armies, the paternalistic and deeply conservative figure of Pétain appeared to be a Catholic saviour who would restore the traditional values spurned by the secular Third Republic. The authority of the Vichy government extended only over southern France and many of the principal bastions of French Catholicism (notably Brittany, Alsace and Lorraine) remained under German military rule. Nevertheless, the Church lent its unambivalent support to the regime. The hierarchy, led by Cardinal Suhard of Paris and Cardinal Gerlier of Lyon, gave public and private encouragement to Pétain, while the parish clergy were among the most zealous and uncritical propagandists for his promised 'national revolution'.

In return, the Vichy regime rapidly provided ample proof of its readiness to serve Catholic interests. Freemasonry was forcibly dissolved, Catholic youth organisations were encouraged, official support for Catholic schools was increased and religious education introduced into state schools. It was, however, above all by its symbolism and language that the new regime displayed its Catholic credentials. As in Austria during the Dollfuss–Schuschnigg years or in Francoist Spain, Pétain and his colleagues exalted the role of the Church and of Catholic morality. The clergy were omnipresent at official events and a suffocating rhetoric of Catholic platitudes suffused the regime's propaganda. The new France that would arise from the ashes of defeat would be one refashioned in the image of a nostalgic and traditionalist Catholic piety: the young were exhorted to respect their elders and love their nation, women should devote themselves to the private virtues of home and family, and employers and workers must work together for the good of the national community.

One had to search hard in 1940 to find Catholics immune to the appeals of Pétain's regime. Even among many of those who before 1940 had advocated Christian democratic ideas, there was an optimistic conviction that the new regime would bring about a social and political system based on Catholic values. There were certainly some seeds of doubt. The decision of the new regime not merely to accept the German hegemony but to pursue, almost in a spirit of penance for past sins, a policy of collaboration with the German victors aroused Catholic fears of the importation of so-called pagan Nazi values into France. Moreover, even within the structures of Vichy the ascendancy of Catholic values was not assured. The new regime was a chaotic amalgam of former critics of the Third Republic, some of whom – such as Pierre Laval, the first prime minister of the new government – were firmly opposed to a clerical hegemony.

Nevertheless, in the summer of 1940, the overwhelming majority of French Catholics placed their faith in the reassuring figure of Pétain. Catholic militants provided much of the personnel of the new regime and Catholics joined in large numbers the mass movements that it established. This unprecedented Catholic political mobilisation is inexplicable without reference to the trauma provoked by the national defeat, but it was also rooted in the historic divisions of French politics. The military collapse in 1940 demanded explanation and in the search for scapegoats most Catholics were content to heap the blame firmly on the Third Republic and its secular values. A strong undercurrent of political revenge ran through Catholic support for the Vichy regime. Pétain was the providential saviour in a moment of national crisis but he was also the means whereby Catholics would finally be revenged for the defeats of the Popular Front in 1936, of the separation of Church and State in 1905 or even of the Dreyfus Affair of the 1890s. For the first time in almost a century, French Catholics appeared to have acquired a regime firmly committed to their interests and, especially at a local level, manifestations of support for Pétain's national revolution frequently took on an air of Catholic triumphalism.

Events in France were echoed in central Europe where German expansionism also brought about the establishment of Slovak and Croatian states which, although they operated under close German and Italian tutelage, enjoyed considerable internal autonomy. Given the intimate interconnection that had long existed between Slovak and Croat nationalism and Catholicism, both states were, not surprisingly, strongly Catholic in character. In Slovakia, the achievement of national independence in March 1939 after the final collapse of the unified Czechoslovak state brought to power a regime dominated by the Slovak People's Party (HSL'S) and led by a Catholic priest, Josef Tiso. The new state took on, in some respects, the air of a modern theocracy. The Catholic clergy and laity were prominent at all levels of the regime, which in its corporatist and educational policies explicitly based itself on the principles of the papal encyclicals. The constraints of war and more especially the increasing influence within the regime of pro-Nazi elements such as the paramilitary Hlinka Guard (Hlinkova garda) gradually diluted this initial Catholic character. Its basis of support, especially among the peasantry, declined steadily and, as the Soviet armies advanced remorselessly towards its frontiers, it was forced to depend ever more explicitly on German support. Nevertheless, even in its final years, the Tiso state remained essentially rooted in the social structures and somewhat parochial mentality of Slovak Catholicism.

The German invasion of Yugoslavia in April 1941 provided the opportunity for the establishment of an authoritarian Croat state led by the leader of the Ustasa fascist party, Ante Pavelić. The new state was eager to make much of its Catholic character, nominating members of the clergy to prominent posts and passing laws against freemasonry, contraception and even blasphemy. Despite these gestures, the stance of the Church hierarchy, led by Archbishop Stepinac of Zagreb, remained circumspect. Although he heralded the achievement of Croatian independence as a manifestation of the will of God, Stepinac was distrustful of the fascist and racist ideology of the Ustasa and throughout the war he maintained a certain distance from the new regime. Few Catholics, however, shared his caution. In May 1941, the Pope accorded a private interview to Pavelić, a gesture that could scarcely fail to be interpreted as indicating a certain approval for the Croat leader. Moreover, within Croatia, many parish priests and militants of Catholic nationalist organisations rallied enthusiastically to the Ustasa state. Amidst the chaos and heightened emotions of war, Catholicism and Croat nationalism became even more inseparably linked. The Pavelić regime consciously exploited this interconnection, initiating large-scale enforced conversions of the Orthodox Serb and Muslim populations of Croatia and Croat-controlled areas of Bosnia-Herzegovina. Catholic priests, including most notoriously Franciscan friars, participated actively in these actions, symbolising the fusion that had taken place between ethnic and religious identities.

Tied to the Axis cause by the circumstances of their creation, the Slovak and Croat regimes had little choice but to persevere with a policy of collaboration with Nazi Germany even as a categorical defeat became ever more probable. Slovak and Croat troops fought alongside the Axis armies not merely on the military fronts but also, during the latter years of the war, within their own territories against resistance movements. Dependent on the declining power of the Reich, they became mere puppet regimes, devoid of a will independent of their Nazi masters and doomed to disappear with the final collapse of the Third Reich. Elsewhere in German-occupied Europe, however, the evolution of the war led to a marked decline in Catholic participation in New Order political projects. As early as the end of 1940, many Catholics both in the Low Countries and in France had repented of their initial willingness to accept the inevitability of the German ascendancy and had withdrawn into a cautious *attentiste* or 'wait and see' attitude. At the root of this change was the gradual realisation during the winter of 1940–1 that the war had not in fact come to an end. The German failure to enforce a British surrender and the misadventures of the Axis armies in the Mediterranean, if they did not yet suggest the possibility of an Axis defeat, nevertheless demonstrated that the final outcome of the war was far from certain. In addition, the oppression and material suffering imposed on the populations of western Europe soon provoked a surge in anti-German sentiments. Active resistance in the early years of the war remained limited to small groups but, none the less, a deep antipathy to the German authorities and to the political ideas that they represented rapidly undermined support for New Order reforms.

The evolution of the war and German policies even eroded Catholic support for the Vichy regime in France. The initial enthusiasm for Pétain had been based on the primacy of an internal French context over international events but, as it became evident that the policies of Vichy would be defined by its need to respond to the dictates of Germany, so hostility to Nazism began to take precedence for many French Catholics over their sympathy for Vichy's national revolution.

This Catholic disengagement from Vichy was a gradual but remorseless process. Throughout the war, much of the Church hierarchy and many Catholic militants continued to share many of the ideas espoused by the Vichy regime and Pétain retained considerable personal prestige. But hostility to Vichy's ineffectual policies and, more especially, its perceived willingness to court Nazi favour led most Catholics to withdraw their support from the regime or even to engage in active opposition to it. Rather than a means of Catholic regeneration, Vichy came to appear as a collaborationist regime increasingly dominated by atheist and totalitarian National Socialism.

The German invasion of the Soviet Union in June 1941 had surprisingly little impact on Catholic attitudes. Certainly for some Catholics who had already opted to collaborate with Nazi Germany, it served as a belated justification for their choice; and in both Germany and Italy it provided a focus upon which Catholic anti-communism and patriotic duty could converge. But in general Catholics in occupied Europe remained unmoved by Hitler's decision to declare war on what had been presented in much Catholic propaganda of the inter-war years as the ultimate evil. Some young (or deeply naive) Catholic idealists enrolled in the volunteer military units that the Nazis created in many areas of Europe, such as the Légion des Volontaires Français Contre le Bolchevisme (French Anti-Bolshevik Legion, LVF) which also received the enthusiastic endorsement of the elderly and intensely anti-communist Cardinal Baudrillart of the Institut Catholique (Catholic Institute) in Paris. But they were few in number. For most Catholics, whatever the strength of their antipathy to communism, Nazism had become the more immediate enemy and the invasion of the Soviet Union came far too late to bind the Catholics of Europe to the Nazi cause.

Catholic political attitudes in German-occupied Europe during the remainder of the war were therefore divided among a small minority who chose to collaborate with Nazism; a second minority – larger in number – who engaged in resistance; and a third group, which in most places and at most times formed the majority, for whom hostility to Nazi oppression and sympathy for an Allied (though certainly not a Soviet) military victory did not lead them to support resistance actions. The collaborationist minority enjoyed a public profile out of proportion to its small size. In Belgium, for example, the largely Catholic Flemish nationalist movement, the Vlaamsch Nationaal Verbond (Flemish National Union, VNV), and the Rexist movement of Léon Degrelle chose to work unambivalently with the German occupying forces. Rexists and members of the VNV were appointed by the Germans to prominent positions of responsibility within the country and fought as volunteers in the German armies on the Eastern Front. Both movements sought to rally support by appealing to Catholic anti-communism but they met with only very limited success. The majority of Catholics were deeply hostile both to the Germans and to collaboration and during the final years of the war became increasingly involved in resistance activities or in the protection of those – such as Jews and workers threatened with deportation to Germany – most directly at risk from Nazi policies.

The situation was much the same in France. While the antipathy felt by most French Catholics towards the German occupiers hardened steadily during the war years, only a small minority pushed forward with collaboration with Germany. Two factors determined the choice of this Catholic minority: the conviction that only Nazi Germany could protect European Catholic civilisation against a victory of the heathen Anglo-Saxons and atheist Bolsheviks; and the belief that the authoritarian Vichy regime within France was the best means of preventing the anarchy of a Communist-directed Resistance uprising. These twin themes were skilfully exploited by Philippe Henriot, a veteran of Catholic Action movements of the inter-war years who, as the minister of propaganda of the Vichy government until his assassination by the Resistance in June 1944, made almost daily radio broadcasts to the French nation. Henriot's apocalyptic warnings played on the fears of sections of the bourgeoisie, deeply concerned by the possibility of a post-war Communist revolution, but few saw their salvation in the collapsing Nazi regime, preferring to place their faith in Britain and the United States as well as the Free French forces led by General de Gaulle from London. Those French Catholics who sided with Germany were therefore a small minority of heretics, rebels against their nation and increasingly against their fellow believers. Forced by the logic of the war into an ever more explicit reliance on the Nazi authorities and obliged to work with the diverse fascist and socialist malcontents who had also chosen to side with Germany, they retained little of their original Catholic inspiration. Instead, they became the mere executants of Nazi repression. Thus, for example, Paul Touvier, the son of a large and austerely Catholic family, who was the head of Vichy's paramilitary force, the Milice (Militia), in Lyon during the final months of the Occupation was responsible for the torture and assassination of Resistance members and for the deportation of Jews to the death-camps in Germany.

There was little equivalence between the minority of Catholics who became involved in the blind tunnel of collaboration with Germany and the other minority of Catholics who participated in anti-Nazi resistance. Catholic resistance was a diverse, often hesitant but, above all, spontaneous phenomenon which, from very limited beginnings, gradually acquired a real significance and influenced considerably the character of post-war Catholic politics in a number of countries. It always retained, however, its initial diversity. The motivations that led Catholics into resistance varied greatly and, although some Resistance groups were clearly Catholic in inspiration, many Catholics worked in Resistance organisations with compatriots (and indeed foreigners) who did not share their religious faith. Catholic resistance therefore took many overlapping but also, in some respects, divergent forms and, rather than seeking to impose on it an artificial homogeneity, it is more accurate to speak of several distinct currents of Catholic engagement in resistance.

One such current of Catholic resistance was primarily patriotic in nature. This was particularly so in Poland, where the peculiar intensity of German oppression reinforced the symbiosis between Catholicism and Polish nationalism. The Church, though much persecuted by the Nazi authorities, remained one of the few means of contact and solidarity within the country and Catholics played a prominent role in the major Resistance organisations such as the Armia Krajowa (Home Army). Such Catholic patriotism was also evident in western Europe, where, for example, the movement Défense de la France (Defence of France) espoused a traditional Catholic-inspired French nationalism. Similarly, the clandestine newspaper *La Libre Belgique* (Free Belgium) and the Armée Secrète (Secret Army) movement renewed the tradition of Catholic resistance established in Belgium during the first German occupation of 1914–18. Though generally right-wing and anti-communist in orientation, such Catholic patriotic groups defined their purpose in nationalist rather than political terms. Rather than fighting for a particular political creed, they regarded themselves primarily as patriotic organisations committed to the military defeat of Germany.

A second current of Catholic resistance was much more political in nature. This was composed of those Christian democrat organisations that, especially in France, had opposed during the 1930s both Nazism and the right-wing authoritarianism symbolised by the Vichy regime. The Nouvelles Equipes Françaises and other pre-war Christian democrat groups, as well as periodicals such as *Sept* and *L'Aube*, provided ready-made networks of contacts out of which many of the first Catholic Resistance groups in France emerged. Along with many members of Catholic trade unions, these Christian democrats were drawn towards resistance as a continuation of their pre-war views. Their opposition to Nazism and to Vichy was, thus, from the outset inseparable from their political vision of a more just society informed by Catholic values. At the same time, however, many of these Christian democrat resistance activists also saw their actions in more spiritual terms. The perception of Nazism as a profoundly anti-Christian phenomenon, already firmly established before the war, was reinforced, not surprisingly, by the brutality of the German Occupation. Confronted by the harshness of Nazi policies and in particular by the anti-Jewish persecutions, these Catholics saw their resistance to Nazism as much more than a political choice. It also became both a religious obligation and a means of bearing Christian witness. As the clandestine newspaper, *Témoignage chrétien* (Christian Witness), founded in Lyon in 1941 by the Jesuit priest Père Chaillet, declared unambivalently: 'as Christians we are at war with Nazism'.

Finally, there was Catholic resistance best defined as primarily pastoral or humanitarian. The sufferings imposed by the German authorities in occupied Europe led both the clergy and laity into resistance actions that were motivated principally by the wish to assist their fellow citizens in distress. Movements of Catholic charity multiplied during the war and, though often ostensibly apolitical, many of these were drawn into active opposition to Nazism. Similarly, Catholic social organisations inevitably became involved in helping those most directly affected by Nazi policies. This was especially so after the introduction of labour conscription measures in much of occupied Europe in 1942 which led to the deportation of large numbers of young men to work in Germany. Catholic youth movements, notably the Jeunesse Ouvrière Chrétienne, responded by helping their members to evade the conscription measures and by establishing clandestine structures of assistance within Germany for those who were deported. Catholics also became involved in assistance for the Jewish populations in the face of Nazi persecution. Anti-semitic prejudices had long been prevalent in many Catholic circles and Catholic support for the Jews during the war was far from universal. Nevertheless, the racist basis of Nazi policies and especially the manner in which those policies were directed indiscriminately against all sections of the Jewish population, including women and children, provoked many individual Catholics into action. Clergy and laity helped to save Jews from deportation and Jewish children were hidden in religious communities and Catholic schools under assumed identities.

It is easy to exaggerate the significance of these resistance activities for subsequent Catholic politics. Especially among historians sympathetic to the Christian democracy of the post-1945 years, there has been an understandable tendency to regard Catholic participation in resistance as the decisive experience that forged a new form of democratic Catholic politics. It must be remembered, however, that it was only a minority of Catholics who participated in resistance activities and that the political consequences of resistance were far from uniform. If it served as the catalyst that led some towards a new and more progressive vision of Catholic politics, for others it served as a reminder of the threat posed by Communist revolution. Not all Catholic resistance groups of the final war years were directed exclusively against Germany and, long before the end of the war, many minds had already begun to turn to the social and political upheavals that, it was widely believed, would occur after liberation.

Nevertheless, the war and, more especially, the involvement of Catholics in resistance activities did contribute to the new political mentality evident in many Catholic circles after 1945. In this sense the war served as a period of internal liberation for many Catholics. The direct experience of German oppression and of the crude authoritarianism of satellite regimes such as Vichy France created a revivified belief in the values of free expression, of participatory politics and of individual rights. Both in resistance as well as in many more mundane areas of daily life, the war eroded the barriers between Catholics and their fellow citizens, encouraging new forms of debate and mutual discovery. The consequence was a new mood of openness and, especially among Catholic intellectuals, an interest in the possibility of political initiatives that transcended the Catholic–secular divide. The experiences of the war years also swept away much of the nostalgic anti-modernism that had surrounded Catholic politics during previous decades. Appeals to an idealised past of rural communities and natural hierarchies disappeared almost entirely from Catholic rhetoric. In their place, Catholic movements and parties shared the general aspiration to build the modern, democratic and egalitarian society that, it was hoped, would emerge from the sufferings of the war.

It was, therefore, not surprising that a number of the new Catholic parties that emerged in Europe during the post-war years should have been able to trace their origins back to the Resistance. In France, the Mouvement Républicain Populaire (Republican Popular Movement, MRP), which emerged as the first major Catholic party in France after the Second World War, was dominated by a Christian democratic leadership who had worked together in the Resistance and who had taken the initial decision to found the party in January 1944. In Belgium, the Union Démocratique Belge (Belgian Democratic Union, UDB), a short-lived attempt at a non-confessional workers' party, was created by Catholic resistance activists in Liège. Finally, in Italy, the Democrazia Cristiana (Christian Democrat Party, DC), despite its subsequent transformation into a conservative party of the centre right, was initially much influenced by the mood of political renewal fostered by the upheavals of the war years. In July 1943 Mussolini was ousted by a coup initiated by the king and army, and the new regime led by General Badoglio concluded an armistice with the Allies in September. While Allied troops took over the south of the country and a new political structure tentatively began to emerge in Rome, the north of the country was rapidly occupied by the German armies, who established Mussolini as the ruler of a puppet state, the Fascist Social Republic. Resistance to the German occupying forces and their collaborationist allies developed rapidly in the major industrial cities of the north as well as in many rural areas. Though largely under Communist leadership, the partisan forces that operated in much of northern Italy during 1944 and 1945 also included many Catholics. Catholic trade unionists and intellectuals in cities such as Milan, Livorno and Florence participated in the local Resistance committees, while in highly Catholic areas of the north-east of the country, such as the Veneto, the partisan units were often organised by priests and by the Catholic social organisations.

Although Catholic involvement in resistance activities therefore had considerable political consequences, its impact was limited to specific areas of western Europe. The Catholics of Germany (and Austria) remained almost entirely unaffected; but so too were those in the neutral states of Ireland and Switzerland. In Spain and Portugal, diplomatic isolation from the Second World War ensured that Catholicism remained rooted in the triumphalist and authoritarian mentalities of the 1930s. Moreover, further east in Europe the war offered little scope for political innovation. In Poland and Lithuania the westward advance of the Red Army during 1944 brought with it not liberation but the replacement of one form of foreign oppression by another. Similarly, in central Europe the final military collapse of Germany during the winter of 1944–5 brought about the demise of the collaborationist regimes of Slovakia and Croatia. Soviet occupation of Hungary and eastern Austria as well as the re-establishment of the multi-ethnic states of Czechoslovakia and Yugoslavia under predominantly left-wing governments placed Catholics very much on the political defensive and led to the prosecution of members of the clergy and laity who had supported the Tiso and Pavelic regimes.

It would thus be misleading to present the new Catholic political attitudes forged in resistance to Nazism as typical of Catholicism as a whole. Even in western Europe, the impact of such ideas was often superficial and for the majority of European Catholics the experience of the war years was characterised more by fear and defensiveness than by optimism for a better future. This was most obviously so among German Catholics. Brief moments of patriotic euphoria in 1939 and 1940 were outweighed by fears from 1941 onwards of the high cost of the war in terms of human losses and, after the defeat at Stalingrad in January 1943, of the consequences of a German military defeat. Above all, there was a fear of persecution by a regime in which the most extreme and anti-Christian elements – notably Himmler's burgeoning SS empire – came to the fore during the war years. The response among German Catholics was to reinforce the mood of internal withdrawal already evident during the pre-war years. The bishops criticised the euthanasia policy of the regime towards the mentally ill in a pastoral letter of 26 June 1941 but in general they preferred to avoid conflict and, notwithstanding acts of heroism by individual Catholics, the German Church made no public condemnation of the wartime extermination of the Jewish populations of Europe. The stance of the Catholic laity during the war years can best be described as stoical. Catholics served loyally in the armies of the Third Reich and, despite the often alarmist reports of the Nazi police, the public mood remained calm in Catholic regions throughout the war. Only in Bavaria, where the Nazi minister of education tried unsuccessfully to remove crucifixes from schools in 1941, did Catholic antipathy to the regime lead briefly to large-scale acts of insubordination. The times were not propitious to Catholic mobilisation and, although a few intellectuals had begun to contemplate the new forms of Catholic political activity that might emerge from the ashes of the defeat of the Third Reich, the priority for most German Catholics was the more personal one of survival.

Both in Germany and elsewhere in Europe, there was a rise in religious practice. The manifold sufferings of the conflict led to increased levels of attendance at church services as well as a more widespread recourse to religion as a source of solace and of protection. In some respects this phenomenon was no more than a short-term consequence of war. As had been the case during the First World War, wartime religion was often crude in its forms and exclusively self-centred in its motivation. Soldiers and civilians alike prayed for protection from bullets and bombs, prompting the Cardinal Archbishop of Mechelen in Belgium to issue a message reminding the faithful of their duty to pray not merely for themselves but also for others. But it would be wrong to dismiss the surge in religious practice as merely an artificial product of exceptional circumstances. During the war years, religion – and perhaps most especially the Catholic religion – protruded more directly into the structures of daily life. Its rituals provided continuity amidst traumatic uncertainty. Its institutions and places of devotion served as centres of sociability, of assistance and of refuge, while its doctrines offered reassurance as well as the promise of a better world.

The cult of the Virgin Mary symbolised both the private devotion and the intensity of wartime Catholicism. As the mother of Christ, the Virgin was the recipient of innumerable private prayers of intercession, and local and national centres of Marian pilgrimage – such as the statue of the Virgin at Le Puy in central France – became the focus of often emotional displays of devotion. The Marianism of the war years was not, however, merely a reaction to uncertainty and danger. The Virgin also served as the symbol of a Catholic alternative to a world of violence and mass destruction. Events such as the extraordinary enthusiasm aroused by the procession of the statue of Notre Dame de Boulogne (Our Lady of Boulogne) through much of France during the German occupation, reflected the hope felt by many Catholics that the end of the war would bring about the return of the world to the doctrines of the Christian faith. The dual character of the cult of the Virgin – expressive both of private faith and of public repentance for the sins of the world – continued into the post-war years. The rapid expansion in Marian movements and devotions during the late 1940s and 1950s certainly owed much to papal support. Pius XII consistently encouraged Marianism, culminating in his proclamation in 1950 of the doctrine of the assumption of the Virgin Mary into heaven. But the post-war success of mass organisations such as the Legion of Mary was primarily the consequence of the emotional centrality that the cult of the Virgin Mary had acquired during the war in the lives of many Catholics.

The political consequences of these religious trends were varied. For some, such as the worker priests in France who during the late 1940s abandoned traditional notions of the priestly vocation in favour of living as workers in industrial suburbs, the religious fervour fostered during the war acted as a stimulus to espouse ideas that, at times, came close to a Christian communism. But among many other Catholics, the war provoked a return to a more traditional and defensive mentality. The manifold horrors of the conflict, as well as fears of its possible consequences, reinforced their conviction that the Church was a bastion of truth in a hostile world. The duty incumbent on the laity was therefore to unite in defence of the Church and to accept the directives provided by their spiritual leaders. The authority of the ecclesiastical hierarchy within Catholicism was strengthened by the war years and it was the willingness of the faithful to follow the instructions of the clergy that goes far towards explaining the electoral success enjoyed by Christian Democrat parties in much of western Europe during the post-war years.

This conservative mentality was reinforced by more worldly concerns. The westward advance of the Soviet armies in eastern and central Europe during the final years of the war and the prominent role played by Communists in the Resistance movements of western Europe could hardly fail to give a new impetus to Catholic anti-communism. By 1944, the threat posed by communism had become an obsessive concern of the papacy. Alarmist messages from the Vatican to the Western Allies, predicting an imminent Soviet conquest of Europe, were reinforced by public warnings to the faithful not to be deceived by communist attempts to present themselves as well-intentioned patriots. It was impossible, the official Vatican newspaper, the *Osservatore Romano* (Roman Observer), declared on 23 July 1944, for a Catholic to be a Communist and the newspaper roundly condemned those left-wing Catholic groups – such as the Party of the Christian Left founded by a group of Catholic intellectuals in Rome – that sought to work with the Communists.

Not all Catholics were initially inclined to heed the warnings of the Church hierarchy. During the period of patriotic euphoria that followed the liberation of western Europe from German control in 1944 and 1945, many Catholics preferred to suspend old prejudices in favour of working with Communists for the common goal of national reconstruction. Such optimism proved, however, on the whole to be very short lived. Soviet actions in eastern Europe and Germany as well as the radicalism of some rank-and-file Communists who adapted only with difficulty to the moderate stance of their leaders soon sufficed to revive old fears, and by the end of the war in Europe in May 1945 a strong tone of anti-communism was already evident in much of the Catholic press. Nor was it merely Communists who aroused Catholic apprehensions. Both the clergy and many lay Catholics feared that the predominantly left-wing governments that came to power in Europe at the end of the war would pursue anti-clerical policies. Although socialist and liberal parties on the whole denied any wish to return to the radical secularising policies of the early years of the century, Catholic suspicions of the atheist and freemasonic influence on these parties remained strong and tempered the willingness of Catholic parties in France, Italy and Belgium to collaborate with parties of the centre left.

The conservative orientation of much Catholic politics of the later war years was also rooted in the social composition of Catholicism. The war gave to Catholic workers' organisations a new prominence and self-confidence but it remained the bourgeoisie and the rural populations who constituted the majority of the Catholic faithful. As had already been the case during the inter-war years, this social imbalance exerted an inevitable influence over the character of Catholic political movements. Middle-class fears of social reforms dictated by working-class demands and resentment among farmers at government policies of requisitioning and price control intended to guarantee food supplies for urban populations were both factors that made themselves felt rapidly after the end of the war and that drew Catholic movements – at times almost unwillingly – towards the centre right of the political spectrum. Both in France and Italy as well as, to a lesser extent, in Germany and Belgium, the predominantly progressive Christian Democrat leaders who emerged at the end of the war found themselves obliged to move to the right in order to respond to pressure from the membership and electorate of their parties.

The impact of the Second World War on political Catholicism was therefore much more complex than is often suggested. In many respects, it appeared to have had the effect of moving the centre of balance of Catholic politics considerably to the left. The authoritarian dreams so evident during the 1930s had been discredited by the events of the war and, outside the time-warp of the Iberian peninsula where the dictatorships of Franco and Salazar remained in place until the 1970s, almost all Catholics accepted democratic political structures. In addition, the pre-war political leadership was replaced almost everywhere by a new generation of Catholic leaders, many of whom had participated in resistance or anti-Nazi activities during the war years and who were sincerely committed to acting as a progressive force within a democratic and pluralist society.

This was not, however, the whole story. The changes wrought by the war were, on the whole, restricted to certain areas of western Europe, essentially France, the Low Countries and northern Italy. In neutral Ireland and Switzerland, the effects of the war were much more muted, while in Germany and Austria Catholic alienation from Nazism provided only a limited current of political renewal. Elsewhere, Soviet occupation and Communist rule in eastern Europe led to the persecution of the Catholic Church and the enforced dismantling of the structures of political Catholicism. Moreover, even within western Europe the transformation in Catholic attitudes brought about by the war was less emphatic than it at first appeared. Behind the new rhetoric of democratic openness, Catholic mentalities and anxieties emerged from the war unchanged and even, in some respects, reinforced. The heightened centrality of the institutions of the Church and the clergy in Catholic life during the war years strengthened the traditional vision of the Catholic faith as a hierarchical community bound together by shared beliefs and interests. Consequently, the goals of Catholic political action during the immediate post-war years were largely the familiar ones of unity and of the defence of the Church and faithful against their manifold opponents. Fears of atheistic communism, actively propagated by the Vatican and by much of the Catholic press, reinforced the power of these appeals for unity. Faced with this supposed peril of left-wing subversion, the protection of Catholic concerns rapidly became inseparable from a wider social and political conservatism. Long before the cold war began to polarise European politics, defence of the Church and of the values of political and economic liberty were already frequent themes of much Catholic propaganda and, despite the initial hopes of many of their founders, the Christian Democrat parties established in much of western Europe after the war rapidly became forces of the centre right. Conservatism and not revolution proved to be the more durable consequence of the Second World War for Catholic politics.

BIBLIOGRAPHICAL NOTES

The wartime policies of the papacy are discussed from different perspectives in Chadwick (1986), Deutsch (1968) and Papeleux (1980). Walsh (1991) and Chélini and D'Onorio (1988) consider the personal priorities of Pius XII. Catholic reactions to the German victories in the Low Countries in 1940 are examined in Smith (1987), Luykx (1996), Conway (1993) and in the important work on the Belgian Church by Dantoing (1991). There is a substantial literature on French Catholic reactions to the Vichy regime. Duquesne (1986) and McMillan (1996a) provide general accounts while Bédarida (1992) and Fouilloux (1992b) survey the historiography. Burrin (1995) stresses the pro-Vichy stance of the Church hierarchy while Clément (1989) and Hellman (1993) provide examples of the enthusiasm of some Catholics for the regime's National Revolution. Halls (1995), in contrast, focuses on the more hesitant stance of Christian democrat movements. Wartime events in Slovakia are considered in Jelinek (1971 and 1976) and Hoensch (1973) and those in Croatia in Alexander (1987) and Jelinek (1980), while Rhodes (1973) provides evidence of the papacy's policy towards the Ustasa regime.

Catholic disenchantment with Vichy is traced in Duquesne (1986), Hellman (1993) and Sweets (1986). Davey (1971) and Christophe (1992) discuss the LVF and Cardinal Baudrillart; Kedward (1989) analyses the example of Henriot; and Rémond (1992b) examines Touvier's wartime actions and subsequent protection by elements of the French Church. Catholic collaboration in Belgium is considered by De Wever (1994), Dantoing (1991) and Conway (1993). Examples of patriotic Catholic resistance are presented by Rollet (1987), Wieviorka (1995) and Verhoeyen (1994). Christian democrat and spiritual resistance is analysed in Bédarida (1977), Kedward (1978), Lagrée (1995) and McMillan (1996a), while Catholic assistance to the Jewish and other victims of Nazism is discussed in Marrus (1989) and Molette (1995).

The change wrought in Catholic political attitudes by the war is stressed emphatically by Fogarty (1957) and in a more nuanced manner by Michel (1988) and Luykx (1996). The emergence of the MRP and UDB is described by Irving (1973) and Beerten (1990) and Conway (1996b) respectively. Ellwood (1985), Ginsborg (1990), Pollard (1996) and Delzell (1961) provide different perspectives on Catholic attitudes in Italy after the overthrow of Mussolini. Lannon (1987) and Gallagher (1996) demonstrate Iberian immobilism, while Crampton (1994) provides a general account of events in central and eastern Europe. The wartime actions and hesitations of German Catholics are discussed by Kitchen (1995), Zahn (1963), Kershaw (1983) and Lönne (1996). Aspects of wartime religious practice are provided by Van Roey (1945), Chélini (1983), Maerten (1991) and Dantoing (1984). Marianism is the subject of Laury (1982), Perry and Echeverria (1988) and Bédarida (1992). Walsh (1991) stresses Pius XII's support for the Marian cult.

Arnal (1986) provides a history of the worker priest movement in France, while papal anti-communism is discussed in Papeleux (1985), Carrillo (1991) and Durand (1991). The complex legacy of the war for Catholic politics is illustrated by Mayeur (1980), Irving (1973), Leonardi and Wertman (1989) and Pridham (1977).

Conclusion

The year 1945 was a turning point, but not a decisive one, in Catholic politics. During the two decades after the Second World War a new and highly successful structure of Catholic parties played a preponderant role in the politics of western Europe. In Germany, Austria, Italy, Switzerland and the Low Countries, Christian Democrat parties rapidly established themselves as major electoral forces and participated almost without interruption in government. Only France, where the spectacular post-war success of the Mouvement Républicain Populaire was followed by an equally vertiginous decline, remained an obstinate exception to this story of success.

There are several explanations for the hegemony of the Christian Democrat parties in the politics of the late 1940s and 1950s. The influence of the cold war and the consequent marginalisation of communism as well as the unprecedented prosperity brought about by rapid post-war economic growth undoubtedly benefited the Christian Democrats. Their commitment to parliamentary democracy and private enterprise combined with enhanced systems of social security and welfare provision was well suited to the conservative and individualist ethos of the era. But it would be wrong to neglect the religious reasons for their success. Although the Christian Democrat parties benefited from the votes of many conservatives concerned to oppose left-wing radicalism, the majority of their electorate was Catholic. As had been the case during the inter-war years, many Catholics during the 1940s and 1950s found it natural to make a connection between their religious faith and support for a political party committed to the defence of the Church and Catholic social and moral values. Reinforced by the bonds of solidarity created by the powerful networks of Catholic social, economic and educational organisations, a sense of a shared Catholic identity was a tangible reality in post-war Europe. The division between Catholic and non-Catholic remained inscribed in the structures of daily life. Not just the rites of passage of birth, marriage and death but also their choice of school, trade union, newspaper and even insurance or funeral company continued to distinguish Catholics from their fellow citizens. Political choice was merely one expression of this wider reality.

Catholic political success after 1945 was therefore in many respects the culmination of the expansion of political Catholicism during the previous decades traced in this book. The development of Catholic politics did not respect the conventional division of twentieth-century European history into two eras divided by the watershed of the Second World War. Instead, the period from the First World War to the 1960s formed a unity, in which the events of the Second World War served more to confirm existing trends than to provoke change. In contrast, it was the 1960s that witnessed a decisive rupture in Catholic politics. The nature of religion was transformed by the social changes of the decade: levels of religious practice fell markedly, many Catholic trade unions and other social organisations broke away from the Church and new forms of social behaviour overwhelmed old moral certainties. Above all, there was a profound change in Catholic mentalities. The Second Vatican Council, the first world-wide gathering of the Church hierarchy since the mid-nineteenth century, organised by Pope John XXIII (and his successor Paul VI) in Rome from 1962 to 1965 introduced major reforms of Church doctrines and structures. The ultramontane fundamentalism and hierarchical authoritarianism of Pius XI and XII were dismantled and replaced by a new vision of the Catholic Church as a community of believers willing to engage with the reality of a more pluralist and secular society.

After the social and institutional changes of the 1960s, Catholic politics could never be the same again. The clergy ceased to issue guidance to the faithful to vote for Catholic parties, while many of the laity no longer saw any natural connection between their religious faith and their political loyalties. The notion of Catholic distinctiveness, of an 'imagined community' of the Catholic faithful united by shared spiritual and political interests, which had provided the driving force behind the emergence of Catholic politics since the late nineteenth century, gave way to a new era of religious and political pluralism. Consequently, Catholic parties could no longer take confessional loyalties for granted and were obliged to find new ways of appealing for the support of the electorate. Legacies of former mentalities certainly remained. In Spain and Portugal, it was only after the democratic transitions of the 1970s that Catholic attitudes shook off the heritage of their authoritarian past. The election of Pope John Paul II in 1979 and the collapse of the Communist regimes in eastern Europe a decade later have brought back into the European mainstream an intransigent Catholicism relatively untouched by the spiritual and political currents of western Europe. The reality of a Catholic Europe still exists and, notwithstanding all of the changes of recent decades, confessional difference still remains one of the most reliable factors in explaining electoral loyalties.

Nevertheless, it is impossible to deny the extent and importance of the transformation that has taken place in European Catholicism since the 1960s. The religious, social and political structures of the faith have all undergone profound changes which, whatever the nostalgia of certain Church leaders, render impossible any return to the assumptions of the past. The structures and mentalities described in this book therefore formed part of a distinct era in Catholic politics which, despite the undoubted changes that took place between 1918 and 1945, were based on a certain number of underlying continuities. Three of these were of particular importance.

The first was the role of the papacy. The first half of the twentieth century marked the zenith of papal power. Both as an institution and as a source of spiritual and doctrinal authority, the papacy exercised a remarkable influence over the forms and character of Catholic belief. The self-conscious majesty of the Popes and the reverential respect that surrounded their public pronouncements served not only to increase their own power but to reinforce among the Catholic faithful of Europe (and indeed beyond) their perception of themselves as members of a Catholic spiritual community which transcended frontiers of nation, ethnicity or social class.

The second continuity was the vision of the Catholic Church as a bastion of incontrovertible truth in an alien and sinful world. Although certain Catholic intellectuals were already beginning to question the authoritarian hierarchy of the Church and some timid ecumenical initiatives towards other faiths were launched during the 1920s and 1930s, the Church remained an overwhelmingly anti-democratic and inward-looking institution, intolerant of internal and external debate. Catholicism was not a community but a hierarchical organisation in which, in the manner of medieval estates, the papacy, the bishops, the clergy and the laity each had their appointed place. Doctrine was passed down from above and the responsibility of the laity was to follow (either literally or metaphorically) as faithful children the injunctions of the clergy. The consequence was a 'ghetto mentality' in which the faithful were enclosed as far as possible within a self-contained network of

Catholic social and cultural organisations, and contact with those beyond the faith was seen either positively as an opportunity for evangelism or negatively as a source of danger, but rarely as an opportunity for mutual discussion.

The third element of continuity was the principles that governed Catholic political action. Although Catholic politics took many forms in inter-war Europe, it remained focused on two central concerns: the protection of the Church and of its affiliated institutions against the attacks of its real or suspected enemies and the implementation of what was felt to be a distinctive and unitary agenda of Catholic-inspired policies, based notably on the encyclicals of the Popes. The balance between these defensive and positive goals varied greatly at different places and at different times. So too did the political orientation of their expression: the largely conservative parties of the 1920s and the authoritarian movements and the Christian democratic groups of the 1930s reflected the often contradictory influences on political Catholicism of wider ideological and social conflicts. Behind such diversity, however, Catholic politics remained rooted in the twin preoccupations of defence of the Church and of the enactment of a particular Catholic vision of society. New definitions of the purposes of Catholic politics made themselves felt tentatively in the 1930s and, more noticeably, during the years of the Second World War. But they remained minority currents, limited on the whole to intellectual circles, and had little impact on the tone of confident certainty that predominantly characterised the Catholic politics of the period.

Based on these three pillars, the history of Catholicism in Europe between 1918 and 1945 was primarily one of successful adaptation to the political and social challenges of the era. Long-term forces of economic and social modernisation continued slowly to erode levels of religious practice in many – though not all – Catholic areas of Europe. This decline was, however, much less marked than among Protestant and Jewish populations and was to a considerable extent compensated for by other developments. The central institutions of the Church increased in importance; Catholic educational, social and cultural organisations occupied an influential place in public life; and the rituals and symbolism of the faith retained an inescapable (though certainly not unchallenged) centrality in daily life. Indeed, in many areas of Europe, Catholicism was manifestly more visible and more assertive in 1945 than it had been thirty years earlier. Above all, its strength during these years derived from the commitment to the faith displayed by the Catholic laity. The willingness of many Catholics to place their religious belief at the centre of their lives provided the Church with an inner dynamism and ensured an almost inexhaustible supply of militants eager to participate in Catholic spiritual, social and political campaigns.

The expansion of Catholic political movements was, thus, a consequence of the more general vitality of the Catholic faith. The perceived need to defend the Church against attack, but also the desire to achieve social and political reforms based on Catholic principles, acted as the driving force behind the many and varied forms of Catholic political action. Not all of these movements shared the same goals. Differences of social class, of historical tradition and of generation had long been important within Catholicism and were exacerbated by the challenges of the inter-war years. Nevertheless, Catholic politics during this period retained an essential unity which renders artificial any attempt to divide it into subsidiary currents such as Christian democracy, Catholic conservatism or clerico-fascism. Just as Liberal, Socialist and even Communist parties united different tendencies beneath a common banner, so Catholic movements of the 1920s and 1930s inevitably comprised elements whose goals diverged and to some extent conflicted. There was no homogeneity, but nor should the existence of conflicts and tensions be allowed to disguise the many points of convergence. All considered themselves to be part of a distinctive Catholic political tradition which had its own values, heritage and objectives. Both within national boundaries and beyond them, Catholic movements formed an important and all-too-often overlooked component of European politics. Without them, the historical picture of twentieth-century Europe is not complete.

BIBLIOGRAPHICAL NOTES

Irving (1979) provides a survey of Catholic politics in Europe since 1945. The persistence of a defensive Catholic mentality is underlined by Altermatt (1989), Bakvis (1981) and, in his interesting comparative study, by Whyte (1981). Weber (1991) is the originator of the term 'ultramontane fundamentalism' to describe papal teachings prior to the Second Vatican Council. Jedin (1981), Hebblethwaite (1994), Fahey (1992) and the essays in Buchanan and Conway (1996) all stress in very different ways the importance of the watershed of the 1960s.

Anderson (1995) applies the term 'imagined community' to German Catholicism. Lannon (1987) and Gallagher (1983) illustrate the time-warp of Iberian Catholicism. Schmitt (1990) and Billiet (1996) analyse the persistence of religious affiliations as a factor in determining electoral choices. Toibin (1994) is a stimulating and perceptive account of travels in Europe's present-day Catholic cultures.

Bibliography

This bibliography lists only those works cited in the Bibliographical Notes. For additional guidance, the reader is advised to consult T. Buchanan and M. Conway (eds) (1996) *Political Catholicism in Europe 1918–1965* (Oxford) and J.-M. Mayeur (1980) *Des Partis catholiques à la démocratie chrétienne* (Paris).

Agócs, Sándor (1988) *The Troubled Origins of the Italian Catholic Labor Movement, 1878–1914* (Detroit).

Agostino, M. (1991) *Le Pape Pie XI et l'opinion publique (1922–1939)* (Rome).

Alexander, Stella (1987) 'Croatia: The Catholic Church and Clergy 1919–1945', in R.J. Wolff and J.K. Hoensch (eds) *Catholics, the State and the European Radical Right 1919–1945* (Boulder).

Altermatt, U. (1972) *Der Weg der Schweizer Katholiken ins Ghetto* (Zurich).

——(1979) 'Conservatism in Switzerland: A Study in Antimodernism', *Journal of Contemporary History* XIV, 581–610.

——(1989) *Katholizismus und Moderne: Zur Sozial- und Mentalitätsgeschichte der Schweizer Katholiken im 19. und 20. Jahrhundert* (Zurich).

Anderson, M.L. (1981) *Windthorst: A Political Biography* (Oxford and New York).

——(1995) 'The Limits of Secularization: On the Problem of the Catholic Revival in Nineteenth-Century Germany', *Historical Journal* XXXVIII, 647–70.

Arnal, Oscar L. (1985) *Ambivalent Alliance. The Catholic Church and the Action Française 1899–1939* (Pittsburgh).

——(1986) *Priests in Working-Class Blue: The History of the Worker Priests (1943–1954)* (New York and Mahwah).

——(1987) 'Toward a Lay Apostolate of the Workers: Three Decades of Conflict for the French *Jeunesse Ouvrière Chrétienne* (1927–56)', *The Catholic Historical Review* LXXIII, 211–27.

Aubert, R., Beckmann, J., Corish, P.J. and Lill, R. (1981a) *The Church in the Age of Liberalism* (London).

——Bandmann, C., Baumgartner, J., Bendiscioli, M., Gadille, J., Köhler, O., Lill, R., Stasiewski, R. and Weinzierl, E. (1981b) *The Church in the Industrial Age* (London).

Bakvis, Herman (1981) *Catholic Power in the Netherlands* (Kingston and Montreal).

Barthélemy-Madaule, Madeleine (1973) *Marc Sangnier 1873–1950* (Paris).

Baumont, S. (ed.) (1993) *Histoire de Lourdes* (Toulouse).

Beaufays, J. (1973) *Les Partis catholiques en Belgique et aux Pays-Bas* (Brussels).

Becker, Annette (1994) *La Guerre et la foi* (Paris).

Bédarida, R. (1977) *Les Armes de l'esprit: témoignage chrétien (1941–1944)* (Paris).

——(1992) 'La Hiérarchie catholique', in J.-P. Azéma and F. Bédarida (eds) *Vichy et les Français* (Paris).

Beerten, W. (1990) *Le Rêve travailliste en Belgique. Histoire de l'UDB 1944–1947* (Brussels).

Ben-Ami, Shlomo (1983) *Fascism from Above: The Dictatorship of Primo de Rivera in Spain, 1923–1930* (Oxford).

——(1984) 'The Republican "Take-over": Prelude to Inevitable Catastrophe?', in P. Preston (ed.) *Revolution and War in Spain 1931–1939* (London and New York).

Billiet, Jaak (1996) 'Les Electeurs du PSC et du CVP', in *Un Parti dans l'histoire: 50 ans d'action du Parti Social Chrétien* (Louvain-la-Neuve).

Blackbourn, David (1980) *Class, Religion and Local Politics in Wilhelmine Germany. The Centre Party in Württemberg before 1914* (New Haven and London).

——(1993) *Marpingen: Apparitions of the Virgin Mary in Bismarckian Germany* (Oxford).

Blinkhorn, Martin (1975) *Carlism and Crisis in Spain, 1931–1939* (Cambridge).

Boulard, Fernand (1954) *Premiers Itinéraires en sociologie religieuse* (Paris).

Boyer, John W. (1981) *Political Radicalism in Late Imperial Vienna. Origins of the Christian Social Party 1848–1897* (Chicago and London).

——(1995) *Culture and Political Crisis in Vienna. Christian Socialism in Power, 1897–1918* (Chicago and London).

Buchanan, T. (1997) *Britain and the Spanish Civil War* (Cambridge).

——and Conway, M. (eds) (1996) *Political Catholicism in Europe 1918–1965* (Oxford).

Bukey, Evan Burr (1986) *Hitler's Hometown. Linz, Austria 1908–1945* (Bloomington and Indianapolis).

Burrin, Philippe (1995) *La France à l'heure allemande 1940–1944* (Paris).

Callahan, William J. (1989) 'The Spanish Parish Clergy, 1874–1930', *The Catholic Historical Review* LXXV, 405–22.

——(1995) 'An Organizational and Pastoral Failure: Urbanization, Industrialization and Religion in Spain 1850–1930', in H. McLeod (ed.) *European Religion in the Age of Great Cities 1830–1930* (London and New York).

Cardijn: un homme, un mouvement. Een mens, een beweging (Leuven, 1983).

Cardoza, Anthony L. (1982) *Agrarian Politics and Italian Fascism. The Province of Bologna 1901–1926* (Princeton).

Carr, R. (1982) *Spain 1808–1975* (2nd edn, Oxford).

Carrillo, Elisa (1991) 'The Italian Catholic Church and Communism 1943–1963', *The Catholic Historical Review* LXXVII, 644–57.

Carsten, F.L. (1977) *Fascist Movements in Austria: From Schönerer to Hitler* (London and Beverley Hills).

Cent Ans de catholicisme social dans la région du Nord: actes du colloque de Lille des 7 et 8 décembre 1990, Revue du Nord LXXIII (1991).

Chadwick, Owen (1981) *The Popes and European Revolution* (Oxford).

——(1986) *Britain and the Vatican during the Second World War* (Cambridge).

Chaline, Nadine-Josette (ed.) (1993) *Chrétiens dans la première guerre mondiale* (Paris).

Chélini, Jean (1983) *L'Eglise sous Pie XII: la tourmente (1939–1945)* (Paris).

——and D'Onorio, J.-B. (eds) (1988) *Pie XII et la Cité: la pensée et l'action politiques de Pie XII* (Aix and Marseille).

Childers, T. (1983) *The Nazi Voter. The Social Foundations of Fascism in Germany, 1919–1933* (Chapel Hill and London).

Christian, William A. (1972) *Person and God in a Spanish Valley* (London and New York).

——(1992) *Moving Crucifixes in Modern Spain* (Princeton).

——(1996) *Visionaries: The Spanish Republic and the Reign of Christ* (Berkeley).

Christophe, Paul (1989) *1939–1940: Les Catholiques devant la guerre* (Paris).

——(1992) 'Le Cardinal Baudrillart et ses choix pendant la seconde guerre mondiale', *Revue d'histoire de l'Eglise de France* LXXVIII, 57–75.

Clément, J.-L. (1989) 'Un Conseiller national de Vichy: l'abbé Louis Sorel (1880–1943)', *Annales du midi* CI, 261–73.

Cohen, Paul (1988) 'Heroes and Dilettantes: The *Action Française, Le Sillon* and the Generation of 1905–14', *French Historical Studies* XV, 673–87.

Comte, Bernard (1985) 'Emmanuel Mounier devant Vichy et la Révolution Nationale en 1940–41: l'histoire réinterprétée', *Revue d'histoire de l'Eglise de France* LXXI, 253–79.

Conway, Martin (1990) 'Building the Christian City: Catholics and Politics in Inter-war Francophone Belgium', *Past and Present* CXXVIII, 117–51.

——(1993) *Collaboration in Belgium: Léon Degrelle and the Rexist Movement 1940–1944* (New Haven and London).

——(1996a) 'Introduction', in T. Buchanan and M. Conway (eds) *Political Catholicism in Europe 1918–1965* (Oxford).

——(1996b) 'Belgium', in T. Buchanan and M. Conway (eds) *Political Catholicism in Europe 1918–1965* (Oxford).

Coutrot, Aline (1961) *Un Courant de la pensée catholique: l'hebdomadaire 'Sept' (mars 1934–août 1937)* (Paris).

Crampton, R.J. (1994) *Eastern Europe in the Twentieth Century* (London and New York).

Cronin, Mike (1994) 'The Socio-economic Background and Membership of the Blueshirt Movement, 1932–5', *Irish Historical Studies* XXIX, 234–49.

Dantoing, Alain (1984) 'La Vie religieuse sous l'occupation', in *1940–1945: La Vie quotidienne en Belgique* (Brussels).

——(1991) *La 'Collaboration' du Cardinal: l'église de Belgique dans la guerre 40* (Brussels).

Davey, Owen Anthony (1971) 'The Origins of the Légion des Volontaires Français contre le Bolchevisme', *Journal of Contemporary History* VI, 29–45.

De Grand, Alexander J. (1989) *Italian Fascism: Its Origins and Development* (London).

De Grazia, Victoria (1981) *The Culture of Consent: Mass Organization of Leisure in Fascist Italy* (Cambridge).

——(1992) *How Fascism Ruled Women: Italy 1922–1945* (Berkeley).

Delbreil, Jean-Claude (1990) *Centrisme et démocratie chrétienne en France: le Parti Démocrate Populaire des origines au MRP (1919–1944)* (Paris).

Delzell, Charles F. (1961) *Mussolini's Enemies. The Italian Anti-Fascist Resistance* (Princeton).

Deutsch, Harold C. (1968) *The Conspiracy against Hitler in the Twilight War* (Minneapolis).

De Wever, Bruno (1994) *Greep naar de macht: Vlaams-nationalisme en Nieuwe Orde. Het VNV 1933–1945* (Tielt and Gent).

Diamant, Alfred (1960) *Austrian Catholics and the First Republic* (Princeton).

Dobbelaere, Karel (1981) 'Secularization: A Multi-Dimensional Concept'. *Current Sociology* XXIX, 1–216.

Dumons, Bruno (1994) 'Prédicateurs et directeurs spirituels des élites catholiques lyonnaises (1890–1950)', *Revue Historique* CCXCII, 95–122.

Dunphy, Richard (1995) *The Making of Fianna Fáil Power in Ireland 1923–1948* (Oxford).

Duquesne, J. (1986) *Les Catholiques français sous l'Occupation* (2nd edn. Paris).

Durand, J.-D. (1991) *L'Eglise catholique dans la crise de l'Italie (1943–1948)* (Rome).

Edmondson, C. Earl (1976) *The Heimwehr and Austrian Politics 1918–1936* (Athens, Georgia).

Ellwood, David W. (1985) *Italy 1943–1945* (Leicester).

Ellwood, Sheelagh M. (1987) *Spanish Fascism in the Franco Era: Falange Española de las Jons, 1936–76* (Basingstoke and London).

Etienne, J.-M. (1968) *Le Mouvement rexiste jusqu'en 1940* (Paris).

Evans, Ellen L. (1981) *The German Center Party 1870–1933* (Carbondale and Edwardsville).

——(1984), 'Catholic Political Movements in Germany, Switzerland and the Netherlands: Notes for a Comparative Approach', *Central European History* XVII. 91–119.

Fahey, Tony (1992) 'Catholicism and Industrial Society in Ireland', in J.T. Goldthorpe and C.T. Whelan (eds) *The Development of Industrial Society in Ireland* (Oxford).

Falter, Jürgen W. (1991) *Hitlers Wähler* (Munich).

Farr, Ian (1978) 'Populism in the Countryside: The Peasant Leagues in Bavaria in the 1890s', in R.J. Evans (ed.) *Society and Politics in Wilhelmine Germany* (London and New York).

Felak, James Ramon (1994) *'At the Price of the Republic': Hlinka's Slovak People's Party. 1929–1938* (Pittsburgh).

Fielding, Steven (1993) *Class and Ethnicity: Irish Catholics in England 1880–1939* (Buckingham and Philadelphia).

Fogarty, M. (1957) *Christian Democracy in Europe 1820–1953* (London).

Fouilloux, E. (1990) 'Courants de pensée, piété, apostolat: le catholicisme', in J.M. Mayeur (ed.) *Histoire du christianisme XII. Guerres mondiales et totalitarismes (1914–1958)* (Paris).

——(1992a) '"Fille aînée de l'Eglise" ou "pays de mission"? (1926–1958)', in R. Rémond (ed.) *Histoire de la France religieuse IV. Société sécularisée et renouveaux religieux (XXe siècle)* (Paris).

——(1992b) 'Le Clergé', in J.-P. Azéma and F. Bédarida (eds) *Vichy et les Français* (Paris).

Furlong, P. and Curtis, D. (eds) (1994) *The Church Faces the Modern World: Rerum Novarum and its Impact* (Hull).

Fusi, Juan Pablo (1984) 'The Basque Question 1931–7', in P. Preston (ed.) *Revolution and War in Spain 1931–1939* (London and New York).

Gallagher, Tom (1983) *Portugal: A Twentieth-Century Interpretation* (Manchester).

——(1996) 'Portugal', in T. Buchanan and M. Conway (eds) *Political Catholicism in Europe 1918–1965* (Oxford).

Gellately, Robert (1990) *The Gestapo and German Society: Enforcing Racial Policy 1933–1945* (Oxford).

Gellott, Laura (1988) 'Defending Catholic Interests in the Christian State: The Role of Catholic Action in Austria 1933–1938', *The Catholic Historical Review* LXXIV, 571–89.

Géradin, Amand (1947) *Notre-Dame de Banneux: la Vierge des pauvres* (no place).

Gerard, E. (1985) *De Katholieke Partij in crisis: partijpolitiek leven in België (1918–1940)* (Leuven).

——(1986) 'Tussen apostolat en emancipatie', in E. Gerard and J. Mampuys (eds) *Voor Kerk en Werk* (Leuven).

Gergely, J. (1977) *A politikai katolicizmus magyarországon, 1890–1950* (Budapest).

——(1980) *L'Influence des encycliques sociales sur les mouvements sociaux catholiques hongrois (1919–39)* (Budapest).

——(1987) 'A magyarországi katolikus egyház és a fasizmus', *Századok* CXXI, 3–47.

Gibson, Ralph (1989) *A Social History of French Catholicism 1789–1914* (London and New York).

Ginsborg, P. (1990) *A History of Contemporary Italy. Society and Politics 1943–1988* (London).

Graef, Hilda (1965) *Mary: A History of Doctrine and Devotion*, Vol. II (London and New York).

Griffin, Roger (1991) *The Nature of Fascism* (London).

Grüttner, Michael (1995) *Studenten im Dritten Reich* (Paderborn).

Halls, W.D. (1995) *Politics, Society and Christianity in Vichy France* (Oxford and Providence).

Hebblethwaite, Peter (1994) *John XXIII. Pope of the Council* (2nd edn, London).

Heilbronner, O. (1992) 'The Failure that Succeeded: Nazi Party Activity in a Catholic Region in Germany 1929–32', *Journal of Contemporary History* XXVII, 531–49.

Heimann, Mary (1995) *Catholic Devotion in Victorian England* (Oxford).

Hellman, J. (1981) *Emmanuel Mounier and the New Catholic Left 1930–1950* (Toronto).

——(1993) *The Knight-Monks of Vichy France: Uriage, 1940–1945* (Montreal and London).

Helmreich, Ernst Christian (1979) *The German Churches under Hitler: Background, Struggle and Epilogue* (Detroit).

Hilden, Patricia (1986) *Working Women and Socialist Politics in France 1880–1914* (Oxford).

Hobsbawm, Eric (1994) *Age of Extremes: The Short Twentieth Century 1914–1991* (London).

Hoensch, Jörg K. (1973) 'The Slovak Republic, 1939–1945', in V.S. Mamatey and R. Luza (eds) *A History of the Czechoslovak Republic 1918–1948* (Princeton).

——(1987) 'Slovakia: "One God, One People, One Party!" The Development, Aim, and Failure of Political Catholicism', in R.J. Wolff and J.K. Hoensch (eds) *Catholics, the State and the European Radical Right 1919–1945* (Boulder).

Holmes, J. Derek (1981) *The Papacy in the Modern World 1914–1978* (London).

Irvine, William D. (1979) *French Conservatism in Crisis. The Republican Federation of France in the 1930s* (Baton Rouge and London).

Irving, R.E.M. (1973) *Christian Democracy in France* (London).

——(1979) *The Christian Democratic Parties of Western Europe* (London).

Isambart, F.-A. (1982) *Le Sens du sacré: fête et religion populaire* (Paris).

Jackson, Julian (1988) *The Popular Front in France: Defending Democracy, 1934–38* (Cambridge).

Jedin, Hubert (1981) 'The Second Vatican Council', in H. Jedin, K. Repgen and J.P. Dolan (eds) *History of the Church X: The Church in the Modern Era* (London).

Jeffery, Charlie (1995) *Social Democracy in the Austrian Provinces, 1918–1934: Beyond Red Vienna* (London).

Jelinek, Y. (1971) 'Stormtroopers in Slovakia: The Rodobrana and the Hlinka Guard', *Journal of Contemporary History* VI, 97–119.

——(1976) *The Parish Republic: Hlinka's Slovak People's Party 1939–1945* (New York and London).

——(1980) 'Clergy and Fascism: The Hlinka Party in Slovakia and the Croatian Ustasha Movement', in S.U. Larsen, B. Hagtvet and J.P. Myklebust (eds) *Who were the Fascists* (Bergen).

Kaplan, Temma (1992) *Red City, Blue Period. Social Movements in Picasso's Barcelona* (Berkeley).

Kedward, H.R. (1978) *Resistance in Vichy France: A Study of Ideas and Motivation in the Southern Zone 1940–1942* (Oxford).

——(1989) 'The Vichy of the Other Philippe', in G. Hirschfeld and P. Marsh (eds) *Collaboration in France: Politics and Culture during the Nazi Occupation 1940–1944* (Oxford).

Kelikian, Alice A. (1986) *Town and Country under Fascism: The Transformation of Brescia 1915–1926* (Oxford).

Kent, Peter C. (1986) 'The Vatican and the Spanish Civil War', *European History Quarterly* XVI, 441–64.

Keogh, Dermot (1986) *The Vatican, the Bishops and Irish Politics* (Cambridge).

——and O'Driscoll, Finín (1996) 'Ireland', in T. Buchanan and M. Conway (eds) *Political Catholicism in Europe 1918–1965* (Oxford).

Kershaw, Ian (1983) *Popular Opinion and Political Dissent in the Third Reich: Bavaria 1933–1945* (Oxford).

Kitchen, Martin (1995) *Nazi Germany at War* (Harlow).

Kohler, Eric D. (1990) 'The Successful German Center-Left: Joseph Hess and the Prussian Center Party, 1908–32', *Central European History* XXIII, 313–48.

Kossmann, E.H. (1978) *The Low Countries 1780–1940* (Oxford).

Lagrée, Michel (1995) 'La JOC en zone occupée, d'après de nouveaux témoignages', in J. Sainclivier and C. Bougeard (eds) *La Résistance et les Français: enjeux stratégiques et environnement social* (Rennes).

Lambert, Y. (1983) 'L'Evolution des rapports entre l'espace et le sacré à Limerzel au XXe siècle', *Annales de Bretagne* XC, 261–72.

Langlois, Claude (1984) *Le Catholicisme au féminin: les congrégations françaises à supérieure générale au XIXe siècle* (Paris).

Lannon, Frances (1984) 'The Church's Crusade Against the Republic', in P. Preston (ed.) *Revolution and War in Spain 1931–1939* (London and New York).

——(1987) *Privilege, Persecution and Prophecy: The Catholic Church in Spain 1875–1975* (Oxford).

Launay, Michel (1986) *La C.F.T.C.: origines et développement 1919–1940* (Paris).

Laury, S. (1982) 'Le Culte marial dans le Pas-de-Calais (1938–1948)', *Revue d'histoire de la deuxième guerre mondiale* CXXVIII, 23–47.

Lee, J.J. (1989) *Ireland 1912–1985: Politics and Society* (Cambridge).

Leonardi, Robert and Wertman, Douglas A. (1989) *Italian Christian Democracy: The Politics of Dominance* (Basingstoke and London).

Lijphart, A. (1968) *The Politics of Accommodation: Pluralism and Democracy in the Netherlands* (Berkeley and Los Angeles).

Lönne, Karl-Egon (1996) 'Germany', in T. Buchanan and M. Conway (eds) *Political Catholicism in Europe 1918–1965* (Oxford).

Luykx, Paul (1978) *De Actie 'Voor God' 1936–1941. Een katholieke elite in het offensief* (Nijmegen).

——(1996) 'The Netherlands', in T. Buchanan and M. Conway (eds) *Political Catholicism in Europe 1918–1965* (Oxford).

Luyten, D. (1990) 'Het katholieke patronaat en het korporatisme in de jaren dertig en tijdens de bezetting', *Bijdragen tot de geschiedenis van de Tweede Wereldoorlog* XIII, 91–148.

Luza, Radomir (1977) 'Nazi Control of the Austrian Catholic Church 1939–1941', *The Catholic Historical Review* LXIII, 537–72.

Lyttelton, Adrian (1987) *The Seizure of Power: Fascism in Italy, 1919–1929* (London).

Maerten, Fabrice (1991) 'La Vie religieuse dans le Brabant Wallon sous l'occupation allemande', *Revue d'histoire religieuse du Brabant Wallon* V, 3–24.

Magraw, Roger (1983) *France 1815–1914: The Bourgeois Century* (London).

——(1992) *A History of the French Working Class*, Vol. II (Oxford and Cambridge, Mass.).

Mamatey, Victor S. (1973) 'The Development of Czechoslovak Democracy, 1920–1938', in V.S. Mamatey and R. Luza (eds) *A History of the Czechoslovak Republic 1918–1948* (Princeton).

Marrus, Michael R. (1989) *The Holocaust in History* (London).

Martin, Benjamin F. (1978) *Count Albert De Mun: Paladin of the Third Republic* (Chapel Hill).

Masson-Gadenne, Catherine (1991) 'Le Cardinal Liénart, évêque social. Action et pensée sociale dans les années trente', *Revue du Nord* LXXIII, 401–10.

Mayeur, Françoise (1966) *L'Aube: étude d'un journal d'opinion 1932–1940* (Paris).

Mayeur, J.-M. (1972) 'Catholicisme intransigeant, catholicisme social, démocratie chrétienne', *Annales économies, sociétés, civilisations* XXVII, 483–99.

——(1980) *Des Partis catholiques à la démocratie chrétienne* (Paris).

McLeod, H. (1981) *Religion and the People of Western Europe 1789–1970* (Oxford).

——(ed.) (1995) *European Religion in the Age of Great Cities 1830–1930* (London and New York).

McManners, John (1972) *Church and State in France 1870–1914* (London).

McMillan, James F. (1991) 'Religion and Gender in Modern France: Some Reflections', in F. Tallett and N. Atkin (eds) *Religion, Society and Politics in France since 1789* (London and Rio Grande).

——(1996a) 'France', in T. Buchanan and M. Conway (eds) *Political Catholicism in Europe 1918–1965* (Oxford).

——(1996b) 'Catholicism and Nationalism in France: The Case of the *Fédération Nationale Catholique*, 1924–39', in F. Tallett and N. Atkin (eds) *Catholicism in Britain and France since 1789* (London and Rio Grande).

Michel, A.-R. (1987) 'L'ACJF et les régimes totalitaires dans les années 1930', *Revue d'histoire de l'Eglise de France* LXXIII, 253–62.

——(1988) *La JEC: Jeunesse Etudiante Chrétienne face au nazisme et à Vichy (1938–1944)* (Lille).

Miller, James William (1988) '*Bauerndemokratie* in Practice: Dollfuss and the Austrian Agricultural Health Insurance System', *German Studies Review* XI, 405–21.

Misner, P. (1991) *Social Catholicism in Europe: From the Onset of Industrialization to the First World War* (London and New York).

Moeller, Robert G. (1986) *German Peasants and Agrarian Politics, 1914–1924: The Rhineland and Westphalia* (Chapel Hill and London).

Molette, Charles (1995) *Prêtres, religieux et religieuses dans la résistance au nazisme 1940–1945* (Paris).

Molony, John N. (1977) *The Emergence of Political Catholicism in Italy: Partito Popolare 1919–1926* (London and Totowa).

Montero Moreno, A. (1961) *Historia de la persecución religosa en España 1936–1939* (Madrid).

Morgan, Philip (1995) *Italian Fascism 1919–1945* (Basingstoke).

Morsey, Rudolf (1977) *Der Untergang des politischen Katholizismus: die Zentrumspartei zwischen christlichem Selbstverständnis und 'nationaler Erhebung' 1932–1933* (Stuttgart and Zürich).

Mühlberger, Detlef (1987) 'Germany', in D. Mühlberger (ed.) *The Social Basis of European Fascist Movements* (London).

Murphy, Francis J. (1989) *Communists and Catholics in France, 1936–1939: The Politics of the Outstretched Hand* (Gainesville).

Neuville, Jean (1959) *Une Génération syndicale* (no place).

Noakes, J. (1978) 'The Oldenburg Crucifix Struggle of November 1936: A Case-study of Opposition in the Third Reich', in P. Stachura (ed.) *The Shaping of the Nazi State* (London).

Nord, Philip (1984) 'Three Views of Christian Democracy in Fin-de-Siècle France', *Journal of Contemporary History* XIX, 713–27.

——(1986) *Paris Shopkeepers and the Politics of Resentment* (Princeton).

O'Brien, Albert C. (1982) 'Italian Youth in Conflict: Catholic Action and Fascist Italy, 1929–1931', *The Catholic Historical Review* LXVIII, 625–35.

Osmond, J. (1993) *Rural Protest in the Weimar Republic: The Free Peasantry in the Rhineland and Bavaria* (Basingstoke and London).

Papeleux, Léon (1980) *Les Silences de Pie XII* (Brussels).

——(1985) 'Le Vatican et l'expansion du communisme (1944–1945)', *Revue d'histoire de la deuxième guerre mondiale et des conflits contemporains* CXXXVII, 63–84.

Pasos, Anton M. (1987) 'La resistencia religosa en la diócesis de Madrid durante la guerra civil espanóla (1936–1939)', in *Les Résistences spirituelles: actes de la dixième rencontre d'histoire religieuse tenue à Fontevraud, les 2, 3 et 4 octobre 1986* (Angers).

Patch, William (1985) *Christian Trade Unions in the Weimar Republic 1918–1933: The Failure of 'Corporate Pluralism'* (New Haven and London).

Paul, Harry W. (1967) *The Second Ralliement: The Rapprochement between Church and State in France in the Twentieth Century* (Washington DC).

Paxton, Robert O. (1987) 'France: The Church, the Republic and the Fascist Temptation 1922–1945', in R.J. Wolff and J.K. Hoensch (eds) *Catholics, the State and the European Radical Right 1919–1945* (Boulder).

Payne, Stanley G. (1980) *Fascism: Comparison and Definition* (Wisconsin).

Péan, Pierre (1994) *Une Jeunesse française: François Mitterrand, 1934–1947* (Paris).

Pease, Neal (1991) 'The "Unpardonable Insult": The Wawel Incident of 1937 and Church–State Relations in Poland', *The Catholic Historical Review* LXXVII, 422–36.

Pecorari, P. (ed.) (1979) *Chiesa, Azione Cattolica e fascismo nell'Italia settentrionale durante il pontificato di Pio XI (1922–1939)* (Milan).

Perry, N and Echeverria, L. (1988) *Under the Heel of Mary* (London and New York).

Pierrard, Pierre (1984) *L'Eglise et les ouvriers en France (1840–1940)* (Paris).

Pinto, António Costa (1995) *Salazar's Dictatorship and European Fascism: Problems of Interpretation* (Boulder).

Pirotte, Jean (1987) *Images des vivants et des morts: la vision du monde propagée par l'imagerie de dévotion dans le Namurois 1840–1965* (Louvain-la-Neuve and Brussels).

Pollard, John (1985) *The Vatican and Italian Fascism 1929–1932* (Cambridge).

——(1990) 'Conservative Catholics and Italian Fascism: The Clerico-Fascists', in M. Blinkhorn (ed.) *Fascists and Conservatives: The Radical Right and the Establishment in Twentieth-Century Europe* (London).

——(1996) 'Italy', in T. Buchanan and M. Conway (eds) *Political Catholicism in Europe 1918–1965* (Oxford).

Polonsky, Antony (1972) *Politics in Independent Poland 1921–1939* (Oxford).

Poulat, Emile (1975) 'Pour une nouvelle compréhension de la démocratie chrétienne', *Revue d'histoire ecclésiastique* LXX, 5–38.

——(1977) *Eglise contre bourgeoisie* (Tournai).

Preston, Paul (ed.) (1984) *Revolution and War in Spain 1931–1939* (London and New York).

——(1993) *Franco: A Biography* (London).

——(1994) *The Coming of the Spanish Civil War: Reform, Reaction and Revolution in the Second Republic* (2nd edn, London and New York).

Pridham, Geoffrey (1977) *Christian Democracy in Western Germany* (London).

Przeciszewski, M. (1988) 'L'association catholique de la jeunesse académique "Odrodzenie" (La Renaissance): aperçu historique', *Revue du Nord* LXX, 333–47.

Rath, R. John (1971) 'Authoritarian Austria', in P. Sugar (ed.) *Native Fascism in the Successor States* (Santa Barbara).

Régnier, Jérôme (1991) 'Diffusion et interprétation de Quadragesimo Anno', *Revue du Nord* LXXIII, 357–63.

Rémond, René (1960) *Les Catholiques, le communisme et les crises 1929–1939* (Paris).

——(ed.) (1992a) *Histoire de la France religieuse IV. Société sécularisée et renouveaux religieux (XXe siècle)* (Paris).

——(ed.) (1992b) *Paul Touvier et l'Eglise* (Paris).

Rhodes, A. (1973) *The Vatican in the Age of the Dictators 1922–1945* (London).

Riall, Lucy (1994) *The Italian Risorgimento: State, Society and National Unification* (London and New York).

Righart, Hans (1986) *De katholieke zuil in Europa* (Amsterdam).

Robinson, Richard A.H. (1970) *The Origins of Franco's Spain: The Right, the Republic and Revolution, 1931–1936* (Newton Abbot).

Rollet, Henry (1987) 'Polonisme et catholicisme: l'Eglise et la résistance polonaise', in *Les Résistances spirituelles: actes de la dixième rencontre d'histoire religieuse tenue à Fontevraud, les 2, 3 et 4 octobre 1986* (Angers).

Ross, Ronald J. (1976) *Beleaguered Tower: The Dilemma of Political Catholicism in Wilhelmine Germany* (Notre Dame).

Ruffieux, R. (1969) *Le Mouvement chrétien-social en Suisse romande 1891–1949* (Fribourg).

Sauvage, Pierre (1987) *La Cité chrétienne: une revue autour de Jacques Leclercq* (Brussels).

Schmitt, Karl (1990) 'Religious Cleavages in the West German Party System: Persistence and Change, 1949–1987', in K. Rohe (ed.) *Elections, Parties and Political Traditions* (New York).

Schönhoven, K. (1977) 'Zwischen Anpassung und Ausschaltung: die Bayerische Volkspartei in der Endphase der Weimarer Republik 1932/33', *Historische Zeitschrift* CCXXIV, 340–78.

Schuck, Michael J. (1991) *That They Be One: The Social Teaching of the Papal Encyclicals 1740–1989* (Washington DC).

Seidman, Michael (1991) *Workers against Work: Labor in Paris and Barcelona during the Popular Fronts* (Berkeley).

Sheehan, James J. (1978) *German Liberalism in the Nineteenth Century* (London).

Smith, M.L. (1987) 'Neither Resistance nor Collaboration: Historians and the Problem of the *Nederlandse Unie*', *History* LXXII, 251–78.

Soucy, Robert (1995) *French Fascism: The Second Wave, 1933–1939* (New Haven and London).

Sperber, J. (1984) *Popular Catholicism in Nineteenth-Century Germany* (Princeton).

——(1991) *Rhineland Radicals: The Democratic Movement and the Revolution of 1848–1849* (Princeton).

Stehlin, S. (1983) *Weimar and the Vatican 1919–1933* (Princeton).

——(1994) 'The Emergence of a New Vatican Diplomacy during the Great War and its Aftermath, 1914–1929', in P. Kent and J. Pollard (eds) *Papal Diplomacy in the Modern Age* (Westport, Conn. and London).

Stengers, Jean (1965) 'Belgium', in H. Rogger and E. Weber (eds) *The European Right: A Historical Profile* (London).

Sternhell, Zeev (1978) *La Droite révolutionnaire, 1885–1914: les origines françaises du fascisme* (Paris).

——(1986) *Neither Right nor Left: Fascist Ideology in France* (Berkeley).

Sweets, John F. (1986) *Choices in Vichy France: The French under Nazi Occupation* (New York and Oxford).

Terrenoire, Jean-Paul (1994) 'Pratique religieuse des catholiques en France: approches sociologiques globales et espaces de référence (1930–1980)', *Archives de sciences sociales des religions* LXXXVII, 153–87.

Toibin, Colm (1994) *The Sign of the Cross: Travels in Catholic Europe* (London).

Tranvouez, Y. (1983a) 'Le Rétablissement des processions sur la voie publique à Lambézellec (1932–1938)', *Annales de Bretagne* XC, 157–69.

——(1983b) 'Images catholiques du communisme français à la fin des années trente', paper presented at the colloquium 'Le Parti Communiste Français de la fin de 1938 à la fin de 1941' (Paris).

Trimouille, Pierre (1991) 'La Bourgeoisie Chrétienne du Nord', *Revue du Nord* LXXIII, 417–27.

Van Molle, L. (1989) *Katholieken en landbouw. Landbouwspolitiek in België, 1884–1914* (Leuven).

Van Roey, Cardinal J.-E. (1945) *Directives religieuses pour l'heure présente* (Brussels).

Vardys, V. Stanley (ed.) (1965) *Lithuania under the Soviets: Portrait of a Nation, 1940–1965* (New York).

——(1978) *The Catholic Church, Dissent and Nationality in Soviet Lithuania* (Boulder).

Verhoeyen, Etienne (1994) *La Belgique occupée: de l'an 40 à la libération* (Brussels).

Vincent, Mary (1989) 'The Spanish Church and the Popular Front: The Experience of Salamanca Province', in M. Alexander and H. Graham (eds) *The French and Spanish Popular Fronts: Comparative Perspectives* (Cambridge).

——(1996a) 'Spain', in T. Buchanan and M. Conway (eds) *Political Catholicism in Europe 1918–1965* (Oxford).

——(1996b) *Catholicism in the Second Spanish Republic: Religion and Politics in Salamanca 1930–1936* (Oxford).

Von Hehl, Ulrich (1987) *Wilhelm Marx, 1863–1946: eine politische Biographie* (Mainz).

——(1992) 'Die Kirchen in der NS-Diktatur: zwischen Anpassung,

Selbstbehauptung und Widerstand', in K.D. Bracher, M. Funke and H.A. Jacobsen (eds) *Deutschland 1933–1945: neue Studien zur nationalsozialistischen Herrschaft* (Düsseldorf).

Von Klemperer, K. (1972) *Ignaz Seipel: Christian Statesman in a Time of Crisis* (Princeton).

Von Rauch, Georg (1974) *The Baltic States: The Years of Independence* (London).

Vos, Louis (1982) *Bloei en ondergang van het AKVS*, Vol. II (Leuven).

Walsh, Michael J. (1991) 'Pius XII', in A. Hastings (ed.) *Modern Catholicism: Vatican II and After* (London and New York).

Weber, C. (1991) 'Ultramontanismus als katholischer Fundamentalismus', in W. Loth (ed.) *Deutsche Katholizismus im Umbruch zur Moderne* (Stuttgart).

Weber, Eugen Joseph (1962) *Action Française: Royalism and Reaction in Twentieth Century France* (Stanford).

Webster, Richard A. (1960) *The Cross and the Fasces: Christian Democracy and Fascism in Italy* (Stanford).

Weinzierl, Erika (1987) 'Austria: Church, State, Politics and Ideology 1919–1938', in R.J. Wolff and J.K. Hoensch (eds) *Catholics, the State and the European Radical Right 1919–1945* (Boulder).

Wheeler, D.L. (1978) *Republican Portugal: A Political History 1910–1926* (Madison and London).

Whyte, John H. (1981) *Catholics in Western Democracies: A Study in Political Behaviour* (Dublin).

Wieviorka, Olivier (1995) *Une Certaine Idée de la Résistance: Défense de la France 1940–1949* (Paris).

Winock, Michel (1975) *Histoire politique de la revue 'Esprit' 1930–1950* (Paris).

Wintle, Michael (1987) *Pillars of Piety: Religion in the Netherlands in the Nineteenth Century* (Hull).

Wolff, R.J. and Hoensch, J.K. (eds) (1987) *Catholics, the State and the European Radical Right 1919–1945* (Boulder).

Zahn, Gordon Charles (1963) *German Catholics and Hitler's Wars: A Study in Social Control* (London and New York).

Zarnowska, Anna (1991) 'Religion and Politics: Polish Workers c. 1900', *Social History* XVI, 299–316.

Zofka, Zdenek (1986) 'Between Bauernbund and National Socialism: The Political Reorientation of the Peasants in the Final Phase of the Weimar Republic', in T. Childers (ed.) *The Formation of the Nazi Constituency 1919–1933* (London and Sydney).

Index

Acción Popular (AP) 57
Action Française 25, 33, 40–1, 72
Action Libérale Populaire 25
Alexander, King of Yugoslavia 56–7
Alsace 81
anarchism 12, 68
Andalusia 12, 69
Anschluss 60
anti-clericalism 9, 12, 13–14, 20–1,
    26, 37, 57, 58, 64, 68, 71, 79, 93
anti-communism 9, 52, 65, 68, 69–70,
    71–2, 79, 85, 86, 87, 89, 93, 95
anti-semitism 24, 63, 64, 88; *see also*
    holocaust
Armée Secrète 87
Armia Krajowa 87
associationism, Catholic structures of
    2–3, 17–18, 36, 65, 97
Ateitis 56
Aube L' 40, 53, 71, 72, 87
Austria 5–6, 11, 24–5, 34, 48–9, 58,
    60, 63, 73, 90, 94, 97
authoritarianism 7, 8–9, 33, 34,
    48–50, 52–61, 72, 73–4, 81–4, 94

Badoglio, General 90
Balbo, Italo 64
Banneux 17
Barcelona 14, 68
Basque country 13, 17, 57–8, 68, 70
Baudrillart, Cardinal 85
Bavaria 24, 35, 66, 91
Bayerische Volkspartei (BVP) 35, 51
Beauraing 17
Belgium 6, 11, 17, 22, 24, 25, 26,
    33–4, 38, 39, 41, 42, 48, 53, 62,

73–4, 80–1, 85–6, 87, 89, 93, 94;
    see also Low Countries
Benedict XV, Pope 30
Black Forest 50
Bloy, Léon 43
Blueshirts 54
Blum, Léon 71
Bosnia-Herzegovina 11, 84
Boulogne, Notre Dame de 92
Britain 11, 14, 16, 70
Brittany 13, 81
Brüning, Heinrich 50–1

Cantabria 17
Cardijn, Joseph 39
Castille 69
Catalonia 57
Catholic Action 7, 39, 40, 41–4, 52,
    55, 57, 60, 62, 64, 65, 86
Catholic Party (Belgium) 22, 25, 26,
    34, 39, 43, 48
Centre Party (Germany) 22, 25, 26,
    34–6, 38, 43, 49–52
Centro Academica da Democraçia
    Cristão (CADC) 59
Centro Católico Portuguesa
    (CCP) 59
Cerejeira, Archbishop 59
Chaillet, Père 88
Christ the King, cult of 42
christian democracy 7, 9, 23–4, 26,
    33, 34, 39–40, 48, 52, 53, 55, 58,
    71, 72, 74, 87–8, 89, 101
Christian Democrat parties 9, 24, 39,
    89–90, 93, 94, 95, 97–8

Christian Social Party (Austria) 24–5, 34, 48–9
Christlich-Soziale Partei *see* Christian Social Party
Christus Rex *see* Rex
Chrzescjanska Demokracja 32
clergy, role in politics 5, 23, 24, 32, 56, 81–2, 83–4, 98
clerico-fascism 65, 101
Coimbra 42, 59
cold war 95, 97
collaboration (during the Second World War) 9, 82, 83–4, 85–6
Combes, Emile 26
communism 5, 6, 9, 61, 68, 71–2, 79, 90, 92, 93, 101
concordats 41, 52, 59, 64, 65
Confederación Española de Derechas Autónomas (CEDA) 57, 58, 67
Confédération Française du Travail Catholique (CFTC) 38
Confederazione Italiana dei Lavoratori (CIL) 31, 38
corporatism 52, 54, 55, 58, 59, 62–3, 81, 83
Cosgrave, William T. 54
Croatia 9, 17, 56–7, 79, 83–4, 90
Croatian Peasants' Party (HSS) 56
Cumann na nGaedheal 32, 54
Czechoslovakia 11, 56, 83, 90; *see also* Slovakia

De Castelnau, General 33
Défense de la France 87
De Gaulle, General 86
Degrelle, Léon 53, 73, 85
Democrazia Cristiana (DC) 65, 90
De Mun, Albert 22, 25
Deutscher Gewerkschaftsbund (DGB) 34–5, 38, 49, 51
Deutschnationale Volkspartei (DNVP) 36
De Valera, Éamon 54
Divini Redemptoris 70
Dmowski, Roman 32
Dollfuss, Engelbert 49, 58, 60
Dreyfus Affair 26, 82

economic depression of the 1930s 7, 47, 48–9, 52, 62

ecumenicalism 99
education 7–8, 42–3, 81
enabling law (Germany) 51–2
encyclicals 8, 21, 23–4, 62, 70, 83, 100
Erzberger, Matthias 34
Esprit 53, 62, 71
Ethiopia, invasion of 65
euthanasia 66, 91
Ezkioga 17, 57

Falange 68
Farinacci, Roberto 64
farmers' organisations 6, 7, 18, 23, 24, 30, 35, 41, 48, 51, 57; *see also* rural politics and religion
fascism 8, 47, 53, 60–1, 63–4, 73
Fascist Party (Italy) 31–2, 63–5
Fascist Social Republic (Italy) 90
Fatherland Front (Austria) 60
Fatima 3, 17, 59
Fédération Nationale Catholique 33
Fédération Républicaine 72
Federazione Universitari Cattolici Italiani (FUCI) 65
Fianna Fáil 32, 54
Fine Gael 54
First World War 30, 36–8
Flemish nationalism 48, 53, 85–6
Florence 90
France 3, 4, 6, 8, 11, 13, 14, 16, 18, 20, 21, 22, 23, 24–5, 26, 27, 32–3, 37, 38, 39, 40–1, 53, 62, 70, 71–2, 81–3, 84–5, 86, 87, 88, 89, 92, 93, 94, 97
France catholique, La 71
Franciscan order 84
Franco, General Francisco 67, 68, 69, 70
freemasonry 13–14, 68, 71, 81, 83, 93
French revolution (1789) 20
Fulda Bishops Conference 65

Galicia 3, 13
Garibaldi, Giuseppe 21
Gay, Francisque 72
Gemeenschap 53
Gerlier, Cardinal 81
Germany 4, 5–6, 7, 8, 11, 18, 20–1, 22, 23, 24, 25, 26, 34–6, 37, 41,

49–52, 61, 63–4, 65–7, 85, 90, 91, 94, 97
Gesamtverband der christlichen Gewerkschaften Deutschlands (GcG) 23
Graves de Communi 24
Great Britain *see* Britain
Guernica 70

Habsburg Empire 22, 32, 34; *see also* Austria, Hungary *and* Croatia
Heimwehr 34, 49
Henriot, Philippe 86
Himmler, Heinrich 91
Hinsley, Cardinal 70
Hitler, Adolf 51, 65, 66
Hlinka, Andrej 56
Hlinkova garda 83
Hlinkova slovenská l'udová strana (HSL'S) *see* Slovak People's Party
holocaust 11, 80, 86, 88, 91; *see also* anti-semitism
Hrvatska Seljacka Stranka (HSS) *see* Croatian Peasants' Party
Hrvatski Katolicki Pokret (HKP) 57
Hungary 11, 41, 90

intellectuals 6, 7, 19, 23, 25, 39–40, 42–3, 53, 55, 68, 70, 71, 72, 89, 90, 91, 93, 99
Ireland 11, 13, 14, 18, 32, 53–4, 79, 90, 94
Irish Christian Front 54
Islam 11, 84
Italy, 6, 11, 12, 21, 22, 23, 24, 25, 26–7, 30–2, 38, 41, 63–5, 85, 89–90, 93, 94, 97

Jeunesse Ouvrière Chrétienne (JOC) 39, 88
John XXIII, Pope 98
John Paul II, Pope 2, 98–9
judaism 1, 11, 100

Kaas, Ludwig 49
Kaunas 42
Konservative Volkspartei 25, 55
Kristallnacht 66
Krizari 57
Kulturkampf 25, 35

laïcité 20
laity, role in politics 5, 22, 24–5, 41–4, 98, 100–1
Lamennais, Félicité de 21
Lateran Treaties 64, 65
Laval, Pierre 82
Le Puy 92
Légion des Volontaires Français contre le Bolchevisme (LVF) 85
Legion of Mary 92
Leo XIII, Pope 23–4, 62
Léopold III, King of the Belgians 81
liberal catholicism 22
liberalism 1, 5, 6, 12, 13–14, 20–1, 37, 43, 53, 62, 69, 73, 93, 101
Libre Belgique, La 87
Liège 89
Liénart, Cardinal 39
Lietuviu Krikscioniu Demokratu Sajunga 32
Ligue Démocratique Belge 24
Lille 39
Lisbon 59
Lithuania 7, 11, 32, 42, 55–6, 90
Livorno 90
Lombardy 30
Lorraine 81
Lourdes 3, 17
Louvain 42, 53
Low Countries 4, 7, 18, 22, 27, 97; *see also* Belgium *and* the Netherlands
lower middle class 24
Lublin 42
Lueger, Karl 24–5
Lyon 81, 86, 88

Madrid 68
main tendue 71
marianism 15, 17, 36, 42, 57, 59, 67, 92
Maritain, Jacques 43
Marpingen 17, 67
Marx, Wilhelm 35, 49
Maurras, Charles 25, 33, 41
Mechelen 91
Michaelists 38–9
middle class 6, 7, 13–14, 22, 32, 34, 48, 50, 65, 68, 69, 72, 86, 94
Miglioti, Guido 31
Milan 90

Milice 86
Mit brennender Sorge 66
Mitterrand, François 72
Mounier, Emmanuel 53
Mouvement Républicain Populaire
     (MRP) 89, 97
Munich 66, 80
Mussolini, Benito 31, 32, 64–5, 90

Narodowa Demokracja 32, 55
National Front (Switzerland) 55
Nationalsozialistische Deutsche
     Arbeiterpartei (NSDAP) *see*
     nazism
Navarre 69
nazism 8, 50–2, 60. 61, 63–4, 65–7,
     80, 82, 85–6, 88, 91
Nederlandse Unie 81
neo-Thomism 43
Netherlands, the 5–6, 11, 25, 26, 32,
     38–9, 42, 53, 70, 80–1; *see also*
     Low Countries
Nijmegen 42
Non Abbiamo Bisogno 61, 64
Nouvelles Equipes Françaises 72, 87

Odrodzenie 55
O'Duffy, General Eoin 54
old catholics (Germany) 21
Opus Dei 17
orthodoxy 1, 11, 34
Osservatore Romano 93

Palatinate 35, 50
papacy 2, 3, 5, 19, 21, 22, 23–4, 25,
     31, 40–1, 52, 54, 59, 60, 64, 65, 70,
     73, 79–80, 92. 98, 99
Papal States 21
Paris 16, 22, 81, 85
Parti Démocrate Populaire (PDP) 33,
     53, 71, 72
Partido Nacionalista Vasco (PNV)
     57–8, 68
Partido Social Popular (PSP) 33, 57
Partito Popolare Italiano (PPI) 30–2,
     40, 65
Party of the Christian Left
     (Rome) 93
Paul VI, Pope 98
Pavelić, Ante 56, 83–4, 90

Pétain, Maréchal 72, 80, 81–3, 84–5
pilgrimages 3, 17, 40, 67
Pilsudski, Marshal 32, 55
Pius IX, Pope 21
Pius XI, Pope 5, 40–2, 57, 60, 61, 62,
     64, 66, 79
Pius XII, Pope 79–80, 83, 92
Poland 11, 13, 32, 41, 42, 55, 70, 79,
     87, 90; *see also* Upper Silesia
popular front: in France 8, 71–2, 82;
     in Spain 68
Portugal 3, 7, 11, 21, 26, 37, 42, 58–9,
     63, 73, 79, 90, 94, 98
press 4, 6, 8, 19, 43, 53, 61, 65, 70, 71,
     93, 95
Primo de Rivera, General 33, 57
protestantism 1, 2, 11, 67, 100
Prussia 35

Quadragesimo Anno 54, 62
Quas Primas 42

religious belief, nature of 1–4, 11–19,
     21, 35–6, 40, 74, 91–2, 98, 100
Rerum Novarum 23–4, 62
resistance (during the Second World
     War) 9, 86–90
Rex 48, 53, 62, 73–4, 85–6
Rhineland 3, 14, 66
Robles, Gil 67
Rome 80, 90, 93, 98
Rooms Katholieke Staats Partij
     (RKSP) 32, 39
Ruhr 39
rural politics and religion 7, 13, 16,
     26, 34, 35, 38, 49, 50, 68, 69, 72,
     94; *see also* farmers' organisations

sacred heart, cult of 17, 36
Salazar, António de Oliveira 58–9
Sangnier, Marc 25, 53
Second Vatican Council 98
Second World War 8–9, 78–95
secularisation 1, 15–16
Seipel, Ignaz 34, 49
Sept 53, 71, 87
Sillon, Le 25
Slovak People's Party (HSL'S) 56,
     73, 83
Slovakia 9, 18, 56, 73, 79, 83, 84, 90

Smetona, Antanas 55
social catholicism 22–4, 39, 54, 63
social class (conflicts within
   Catholicism) 3, 13–14, 32, 44, 48,
   94, 101
socialism 1, 5, 6, 12, 14, 21, 27, 34,
   36, 37, 49, 71, 93, 101
Spain 3, 6, 11, 12–13, 16, 17, 21, 22,
   33, 37, 38, 47, 57–8, 67–9, 79, 90,
   94, 98
Spanish Civil War 8, 47, 65,
   68–71, 72
Stegerwald, Adam 34–5, 38, 51
Stepinac, Archbishop 57, 83
Sternhell, Zeev 61
students 6, 7, 41, 50, 53, 55, 65, 67
Sturzo, (Don) Luigi 30, 31
Suhard, Cardinal 81
Summi Pontificatus 80
Switzerland 11, 25, 26, 54–5, 79, 90,
   94, 97
Syllabus of Errors 21

Témoignage chrétien 88
Terre nouvelle 71
Thérèse of Lisieux, St. 15
Thomas Aquinas, St. 43
Thorez, Maurice 71
Tiso, Josef 83, 90
totalitarianism, Catholic attitudes to
   61, 62, 64, 70, 80, 85
Touvier, Paul 86
trade unions 3, 6, 14, 17, 23, 30, 31,
   34–5, 38–9, 49, 50, 52, 63, 81, 87,
   90, 98; *see also* working class
Turin programme 24

Ubi Arcano Dei 41
ultramontanism 21, 98
Uniao Nacional 59

Union Corporative Suisse 55
Union Démocratique Belge
   (UDB) 89
United Kingdom *see* Britain
universities 42–3
Upper Silesia 14, 39, 55
urban religion 13, 16
Ustasa 56–7, 83–4

Van Duinkerken, Anton 53
Vatican *see* papacy
Vendée 13
Veneto 30, 90
Vichy regime 8, 80, 81–3, 84–5, 86
Vienna 24, 49, 66
Vlaamsch Nationaal Verbond (VNV)
   85–6
Von Papen, Franz 51
Von Schuschnigg, Kurt 60

war, opposition to 74, 80
Weimar Republic 34–6, 49–51, 65
women 3, 14–15, 17, 36, 57
worker priests 92
working class 6, 7, 13, 14, 17, 23, 32,
   38–40, 41, 48, 52, 65, 67, 69, 88,
   94; *see also* trade unions

youth movements 3, 4, 7, 14, 17, 19,
   39, 43, 55, 60, 64, 66, 81
Yugoslavia 11, 56–7, 83, 90; *see also*
   Bosnia-Herzegovina *and* Croatia

Zagreb 57, 83
Zentrumspartei *see* Centre Party